THE GIFT

First published in Great Britain 1973
by Victor Gollancz Ltd
First published in Gollancz Children's Paperbacks 1996
by Victor Gollancz
An imprint of the Cassell Group
Wellington House, 125 Strand, London WC2R 0BB

A catalogue record for this book is
available from the British Library

ISBN 0 575 06297 5

Typeset by Anneset, Weston-super-Mare, North Somerset
Printed and bound in Great Britain
by Cox & Wyman Ltd, Reading, Berkshire

96 97 98 99   10 9 8 7 6 5 4 3 2 1

CONTENTS

1

Granny

Davy Price had first learnt about his gift long ago—oh, he must have been seven or eight, a skinny dark boy wearing brown corduroy trousers with green patches on the knees. No, he couldn't have been quite eight because he still came out of school earlier than the other two, and he remembered that because it had been the first time Mum had got really fed up with Dad—everybody did, in the end—fed up enough to see the kids off to school, and ask the Mum next door to look after Davy until Ian and Penny got home, and . . .

Davy couldn't remember that neighbour's name—they'd moved house so often and had so many neighbours. But he could still see in his mind's eye how her square, cheerful face went blank when Ian had come into her kitchen and said in gossipy tones, "I've come to fetch Davy. Thank you for having him. Mum's run away. She left a note on the mantelpiece for Dad, but I read it."

That neighbour's face had closed the gates of friendliness and become a wall, shutting them out. She wanted no dealings with families whose Mums ran off because their Dads were hopeless.

(Later, after the next few times, Davy had learnt that families with runaway Mums and hopeless Dads wanted few dealings with neighbours. Some might be kind, and some cold, but the kindness was worse than the coldness—eager, inquisitive, excited. Nothing like love. But he hadn't realised that, first time.)

In fact, being not quite eight, he hadn't realised anything much except that he was getting off school for three weeks in the middle of term, and going away on a long, long car journey.

Davy often thought about how they had all changed since then—except Dad, of course. Now it seemed to him that three quite different children had been driven all the way to Llangollen in that smelly old car. (Dad usually managed to change his car at least twice a year, but though they rattled differently they always smelt the same.) Penny had sat in the back, singing to her one-eyed doll. Ian had sat in front talking football with Dad and laughing with triumph when he caught Dad out pretending to have seen some match or player he'd never really seen. Davy had sat in the back with Penny and had slept quite a bit because of the early start, but when he was awake had been caught up in the high spirits of the whole jaunt and perfectly happy.

For Dad possessed a gift, too—not quite as mysterious as Davy's but just as treacherous to its owner. Dad always managed to feel that everything was going to be all right, and somehow made anybody he was with feel just the same. All his schemes would make money, all his smelly old cars were a real bargain, every flitting from house to house was the beginning of a new, rich, carefree life. And he worked his gift hardest when things were at their worst: just after he'd been sacked from his latest job; or when the finance company men had come to repossess the fridge. He'd been like that on the road to Llangollen—probably, Davy now realised, because he hadn't been as sure as he pretended that Mum was going to come back at all, ever.

Only as the long hills of Wales began to swell and swell on the horizon had Dad's high spirits flagged. He fell silent. The late afternoon sun was well to the west, and all the hither slopes were streaked with shadows; Davy became sleepy again, but even as he closed his eyes and longed for the journey to end he saw one of his pictures, a house with a blue slate roof. The wall of the house was low and built of mottled, flattish stones. The windows were small. A woman in a blue dress with a black apron was pumping water into a bucket by the door. It was a picture full of grief, of longing; and with that longing in his mind Davy fell asleep.

"Wake up, kid. We're there!"

(Ian's voice, cheerful and teasing. As it used to be.)

Davy had woken from a nonsense dream about rabbits to the dry-throated discomfort of having slept sitting. He eased his tingling legs to new positions and peered out. Tall hedges screened the sides, and ahead rose an incredibly steep and narrow lane up which Dad's car, smellier than ever, was growling in bottom gear. The engine didn't sound at all happy, and the exhaust behind them swirled dark as a thundercloud. And then the road levelled, the growling stopped and Dad let the car drift to stillness in a place where the lane widened. On Davy's side of the car was a steep field of cropped grass with gorse bushes dotted about it; on the other side were farm buildings and a house with a low stone wall, small windows and a blue slate roof. Not really blue, not as blue as it had been in the picture; dark grey, really, with bluish and purplish tints in different slates. And the woman who stood at the door was wearing a pink dress with a yellow apron and there was no pump.

She stood unsmiling on the white doorstep and watched them climbing out of the car. Davy could smell hot metal, a sharp tang in the fresh hill air.

"You've boiled her dry, Dad," said Ian. "I told you so."

"It's a long way up," said Dad. "Hello, Mam. What've you done with the pump?"

"We have pipes now," she said.

"You got the telegram?" said Dad.

She nodded, and looked in turn at the three children. Davy stared back. Her face was closed. She looked as though she had never smiled, nor ever would. It was a flattish face, wide at the top and pointy at the chin. Her eyes were dark and wide set, her nose and mouth small. Her hair was grey and held into tight curls with a lot of different-coloured hairpins, some brown, some black. She was no taller than Ian.

"We'll have them," she said. "I hope your wife is not sick."

"Rita?" said Dad. "Oh . . . no she suddenly decided that she had to have a holiday. She's had a lot of bother, you know."

It was the first time Davy had heard Dad tell a lie so awkwardly—and it was hardly even a lie.

"Ian," said the woman. "And Penelope . . ."

"Penny," muttered Penny without looking up from her doll.

"Penny it is," said the woman. "And David."

"Davy," said Davy. In those days he had usually preferred to be called David, because it made him sound less babyish. But at that moment he'd copied Penny in asserting his own individuality.

"Who chose it that way?" said the woman, smiling less than ever.

"This is your Granny, kids," said Dad quickly. "My Mam. You're going to stay with her for a bit, till Mum comes back from her holiday, and if you don't treat her right I'll do you."

It was his usual threat, a family joke. There, in the hill lane, in the May evening, it sounded feeble.

"You're our other Granny?" said Penny, looking up with sudden interest from her doll. "Real Granny? Dad's Mum?"

"I am real enough," she said. "You can call me Nain

if you want to tell me apart from your other Granny. That's the Welsh way."

"We'll call you Granny," said Penny.

"We call the other one Granny when she's there and Grumble when she isn't," explained Ian perkily. (That had begun as Dad's way of teasing Mum, but the children had taken it up and now Granny in Watford was more Grumble than Granny.)

"Not respectful, that is," said this new Granny sharply. Her lips stayed straight as ever, but there was something odd about the glance she flashed at Dad.

"Where's Dadda?" he asked.

"Milking," she said. "You come in, children. Tea's been waiting for you two hours."

She turned into the dark doorway. Davy waited for a moment, breathing the hill air that was faintly sweetened with cow-odours, and watching Dad pick a path in town shoes through a miry gateway beside the house. Then he found his way to the kitchen by the smell of new-baked bread.

Dad didn't come in to what this new Granny called tea, but which included boiled beef and apple pie as well as cocoa and doughnuts. They hadn't finished eating when he called from the hall, "I'm off now," and they rushed out into the dusk to say goodbye to him. He rumpled their hair and said to Penny, "Smile, sweetheart, and I'll bring you a new doll when I come back. With two eyes."

"Dolls don't need two eyes," said Penny. You learnt

to answer Dad's promises like that; it gave him an excuse when he didn't keep them and saved you the ache of disappointment. He got into the car and started the engine.

"Lights!" yelled Ian.

They blinked on and moved away. Two seconds later they were gone, screened by the tall hedges.

When the children got back to finish their tea they found their new grandfather sitting at the table, a dark little wrinkled man who smiled at them and said nothing. They were told to call him Dadda.

Five days later Davy had twisted his ankle, badly, climbing in the huge old slate quarry where they weren't supposed to go alone. A few yards down from the farm, on the other side of the road, was a gateway which led into the steep field with the gorse-bushes in it. You climbed up there, panting before you reached the ridge, and suddenly you came to this marvellous place. The grass stopped at a low, ragged wall of stone; beyond that was heather and bent and blueberry scrub covering a broad, moulded spur of the main mountain, Moel Mawr, which hummocked up away to the left. You stood on the spur, gulping the mountain air and looking west across the brown, infolded hills. And at your feet was the quarry.

First, a vast bite had been chewed from the hill-side, leaving a semi-circle of blue cliffs, two hundred yards long and about thirty feet high at the southern end. The floor of the quarry was not flat, but was a series of terraced levels along which little trucks had once run. Roofless sheds and huts stood about. In places you could see where the quarrymen had mined into the hill-side, following the layers of high-grade slate that the shaping pressures of the hills had made there. And from each level, especially below the largest shed, grey screes of waste stone spilt down the slope. When the quarry had stopped somebody had come and taken all the movable iron for scrap—the winding wheels and the engines and the rails—but you could still occasionally find a lever poking through the obliterating grass, or follow the line where some engine had run back and forth and left a trail of still-poisoned vegetation to show its path. The mining shafts had been deliberately caved in when the men left, but it was still a dangerous place. Dadda had showed them why, on the very first day.

He had said, "Will you come with me, now?" and had taken them up the hill and shown them the quarry. Without a word he had led them to the top of the scree below the big shed; he had looked at it, humming, with his head cocked on one side, and then he had taken a fence-post and levered free a large stone near the top. The stone crashed away down the slope, slithering at first, then bouncing in increasing leaps; the stones that it had held in place moved too; with a shuddering grumble the whole surface of the scree had shrugged itself downwards and at last slowly resettled—hundreds of tons of grinding boulders. Grey dust hung above it for a moment, like smoke.

"There is water in the hill-side, you see?" Dadda had murmured when the upland quiet had settled round them again. "The stones are heavy, and the water changes the ground under them, and then they fall. You will not be coming here alone, please. It is a dangerous place, for men, even."

He turned and looked at the jagged curve of the cliffs. Speaking softly as ever he added, "My own brother died in this place."

When Davy hurt his ankle Ian was helping Dadda mend the milking machine. Penny said Davy mustn't go to the quarry, which was another good reason for going, and if he was going to be wicked Penny thought she might as well, too. And then he put his foot into a hidden runner and fell, with his foot trapped fast.

When he finished weeping from the pain Penny ran back to the farm. Davy waited, moaning a little, and at last Dadda walked along the level below him, climbed carefully up and stood looking down at him, shaking his head. His thin arms lifted Davy with no effort at all and carried him back to the farmhouse kitchen. Then Dadda started his old, old Morris up. Granny sat beside him with Davy on her lap and they drove down to Llangollen.

The X-ray showed no bones broken, but the doctor said Davy must not put his weight on that foot for at least four days.

When they got back Granny wanted Dadda to take a strap to Penny for letting Davy climb in the quarry.

"It's my fault," said Davy. "I started it. Penny tried to stop me."

"You're punished already," said Granny.

"If you do anything to Penny," shouted Ian, "I won't forgive you. Ever. Nor will any of us."

So far, from the moment Davy was carried into the kitchen, her face had not changed at all. But now every muscle in it hardened, her mouth became a thin line and two red spots appeared on her cheeks. Davy was very frightened indeed.

"Forgiving and not forgiving," sighed Dadda. "Enough of that we've had, haven't we?"

Granny glanced sideways at him and started to say something, but Dadda sighed again and shrugged and she turned away, biting her lip; she moved the two black swans further apart on the mantelpiece and riddled the range and shifted the stock-pot and turned back to the room. Her face was calm now, but her eyes were still bleak.

"Ian," she said, "will you help Dadda bring the long chair from the front room? Davy must lie up in here, and be company for me. Tomorrow, after tea, Ian and Penny and Dadda will sing me 'All Through the Night'—Ar hyd y nos—in Welsh. Dadda shall teach you and you shall learn, and that will be the three of you punished for climbing in the quarry and speaking so to the woman of the house. Davy is punished already, with the pain and with lying still for four days, when he's here in the hills, in May."

★

The singing went well. Ian had always been in the choir of any school they were at, and Penny could sing on the note. But Dadda turned out to have a voice such as you sometimes hear on a request programme on the wireless when a listener asks for a famous old tenor singing a forgotten ballad, a voice as soft and as strong as the west wind.

"That is good," said Granny, almost smiling. "Hasn't Ian a fine voice? Dadda, when these children go back to England people will be asking them whether they have heard any Welsh singing. Why don't we have a little party, Sunday evening?"

She suggested a few names. Dadda suggested a few more.

"It's going to be a rather large little party," said Ian at last.

Dadda laughed.

So on Sunday morning Granny didn't go to Chapel, but baked instead. Davy lay on the long chair and watched her, very bored. The kitchen smelt sleepy with risen dough and the black clock tocked in its long case and the blue plates gleamed on the dresser but not so bluely as the sky outside, on the hills, where it was May and Davy couldn't go. Granny had sung to him and told him old stories while she mixed and kneaded, so he had been entertained in his mind, but all his body was restless with health and good air and good food, and the restlessness infected his mind and made him bored. And now he was sleepy too with the warmth and idleness and cooking smells.

But he was still wide awake when he saw the picture. It was not part of any dream.

"Funny hat," he murmured.

Granny's hand stilled for a moment at the oven door.

"What's on the mantelpiece?" she said as she opened it.

"Those two black swans, and some brass candlesticks."

"This room, is it?"

"No . . . the mantelpiece is lower and the walls are green."

"But what is funny about the hat?"

"It's gone now. It's all gone."

That always happened when Davy tried to concentrate on one of his pictures.

"But you can remember the hat?" said Granny.

"Oh, it was black and tall and pointy, like a witch's; but she didn't look like a witch. And she had a lace shawl and a black glove on one hand but not the other, and she was sitting in a black wooden chair."

"Yess. Her, that is."

"Who?"

"My Nain. Your great-great-granny. Were you knowing you had the gift, Davy?"

"What gift?"

"It was like a picture you saw of her?"

"Um . . . they aren't quite like that. They aren't flat,

I mean. You can see into them. Why?"

"And they come often?"

"Not very. I don't know. They're only a sort of dream, really. The last one was when Dad was driving us here, and I saw a picture of a house just like this, only there was a pump at the door and the lady who was working it was like you except she had a blue dress and a black apron and her hair was dark. That was funny, wasn't it?"

"Words do you hear, ever?"

"I don't think so. Only sometimes I feel feelings. Why?"

Davy was uncomfortable now. Granny wouldn't answer any of his questions, and her own questions were about his pictures which were part of that private, inside Davy which no one else could ever look at or touch. And besides, there was something about how she was moving and talking. She had taken a sweet cheese flan out of the oven and was simply standing there, holding it, with the oven door open and all the useful heat flooding into the kitchen. Then the flan tin burnt her fingers through the oven cloth and she put it down with a clatter and closed the oven door.

"What gift, Granny?" he said five minutes later. She was working now in the way Mum sometimes worked when Dad had made her cross, as though the busy action of arms and fingers could hush the wild gusts in her mind. Granny didn't answer.

"It isn't fair not to tell me," he said.

"It's not for me to do so, you see?"

"Who shall I ask, then? Mum?"

She stopped beating the white mixture in her bowl, picked up a wooden spoon and with slow, cunning movements eased all the sweet goo neatly into a funnel-shaped bag. Then she bent over a large chocolate cake which Davy had looked at time and again with salivating hunger. When she squeezed the bag a white worm spun itself out of the metal point of the funnel and coiled on to the cake. The coil moved steadily, crisscrossing over itself into a looped lacework, pretty as a flower on the dark brown surface.

"Your mother does not know and would not believe," said Granny with a sigh.

"There's no point in asking Dad."

"Why? No, I do not want to hear . . . So it must be me, Davy. Very well, then. Ten minutes ago I was thinking of my Nain, I don't know why. I saw her in her old Welsh costume that she wore for Chapel on Sundays. When she was a little girl she caught her hand in a chaff-cutter, and wore one glove always to hide its ugliness. All that you saw. She gave me my swans, but the candlesticks she gave my sister who went to Canada. Oh, and your Dad—he was thinking of this house. When I was younger my hair was dark, and often I wore a blue dress with a black apron. Yes, and there was a pump at the door, wasn't there? You saw that too. The day he left . . ."

She paused, intent on the growing lacework of sugar on the cake.

"Why did he leave? Why has he never been back?"

Davy was much more interested in the answer to these questions than in his pictures. He and Ian and Penny had whispered many guesses.

Granny straightened up and glared at him.

"No business of yours," she snapped, before bending to make the worm start winding into a series of little coiled cones.

"But the gift's my business, I suppose," he said sulkily.

"Yes, you have that," she said drily. "It is said to run in your family—Dadda's family. Often it misses a generation. But usually there is one of your blood alive who can see pictures in other people's minds."

"But I *can't*. I mean, if I could . . . well, I'd know what was the matter between you and Dad."

"No," she said. "I knew another Davy that had the gift. He told me that you could not summon it. It comes when your mind is empty. He said it happens like weather. It is always pictures, with no words, like the cinemas when I was a girl—though he could see the colours, of course. Like that it is, isn't it?"

"I suppose so," said Davy unwillingly. It ought to have been exciting, being told he could do a trick like that. But he didn't really like it. And why had he never been told before? And why was Gran making such a fuss about telling him now? He watched her move her icing bag with cunning, careful strokes across the clear space she had left in the middle of the cake. He thought she was writing something, but when she finished she tilted the cake towards him and he could see that she had drawn the bars of a stave and three notes of music.

"That's clever," he said. "It looks scrummy."

"You may lick the bowl, then," she answered.

Granny was a careful housekeeper. On the rare occasions when Mum iced a cake she always mixed too much and left lots in the bowl, but Granny had left only a thin film of piercing sweetness which he could scoop on to his finger and lick off, but nothing he could chew or swallow. It reminded him that there were no sweets in the farm, and the ice-cream van never seemed to pass this way. That was a pity.

"Oh, Davy, Davy!"

He looked up from the bowl in surprise. He had never heard the calm of her voice rumple, even that time when she had been so angry with Ian.

"Don't be unhappy, Granny," he said. "I like it here. It doesn't matter about the ice-cream van. I won't climb in the quarry again, I promise."

She lifted a tray of scones from the oven and moved them to cool on a cake rack, picking each up so deftly that the heat of it had no time to hurt her fingers. Only the last one somehow turned into crumbs in her hand and scattered itself over the pale wood of the table top. She stood looking at the crumbs as though the pattern of them had a meaning.

"Davy, Davy, you're too young," she said. "And I cannot know if I shall see you again to tell you when you are older. So I must tell you now, and you must try not to fret yourself. It is like this—ach, of course it may not be true at all, only a story—but they say in your family that the gift has always brought grief with it."

"Grief? How?"

"The ones who had the gift tried to use it. They saw a picture, and they tried to use the knowledge it gave them. They tried to use the gift. It brought them grief."

"I don't understand," he said.

She stood looking at him, shaking her head. She started to scoop the crumbs on to a plate.

"What happened to the other Davy, then?" he said. "What sort of grief?"

"I cannot tell you."

"I suppose I'll have to ask Dad then."

"No!"

He was feeling sulky again. His lips were fat with pouting. A gift is a sort of a present, and what's the use if people won't tell you about it. It's like being given a new, sharp pocket-knife and then seeing it put away on a high shelf in case you should cut yourself, or your pillowcase, or something. Then he looked at Granny, and saw that her face had gone all knobbly again, as it had when she'd been angry with Ian. But she wasn't angry now. There were no red spots on her cheek. Her lips moved as though she wanted to speak but couldn't.

"What's the matter, Granny?" he said. "I'm sorry."

She made the effort.

"You must promise me, Davy," she said.

"Yes," he said cautiously. "What?"

"I want you not to ask your father about the gift.

I want you not to talk to him about the other Davy. Not ever."

"Then who can I ask?" he said. "I've got to know, haven't I?"

She turned at last and threw the scone-crumbs out of the kitchen door, where her chickens raced chuckling for them. Then she fetched her stool up to the table and settled on to it, and began to twist the wide, whitish ring that she wore on her left hand.

"I must tell you myself," she said quietly. "That I should ever tell it to a child! Like a fairy story! Oh, Davy . . . Well, that other Davy, he was a good man. He worked up at the quarry, because there was not work for two men on the farm, but he lived in this house. Davy was a careful man, and sober always, so they gave him charge of the explosives. Not a lot of explosive you use in a slate quarry, you see, because the explosions spoil the slate, but you must use some. Davy had a mate, Huw was his name. They were like comrades in a story, putting their lives in each other's hands, handling that terrible stuff while the rest of the gangs stood clear. But they were a laughing pair, and handsome. Indeed, when Davy married a girl from down the valley Huw was best man. But then . . . well, two years and three months after the wedding, it was, and Davy was sitting by this fire, tired in the evening, with his wife sewing in that chair, he saw one of his pictures. I do not truly know what the picture was, but perhaps it was his friend Huw lying on a bed, not wearing a night-shirt either, and looking up from the pillow and laughing, and a hand coming into the picture to touch his naked chest. Davy would know that hand by the rings on it. There would be a thin ring of gold and a wide ring of flat silver cut with wavy lines, that had been hundreds of years in his own family. Yes, it was his wife's hand."

Granny was talking to herself now, in a quiet chant, as if she was trying to undo all the old grief by making a magic of it with words. But Davy understood quite well what she was talking about because a year ago they'd been living on a council estate where one of the neighbours had held the police at bay for a day with a shotgun because of what his wife had been doing with another of the neighbours. Mum had talked the story over with friends a hundred times until Davy worked out what it all meant, though he'd still thought it another example of the extraordinary manners of adults. But that had all been fun and excitement. Granny's story was different.

"I told you Davy was a careful man," she said. "He spoke no word that night, and next morning he went up to the quarry as usual. There was blasting to be done that day and he and Huw set the charges. His wife was here in the kitchen, washing his shirt, when she heard the explosion from the quarry. The explosions made a flapping noise always, and shook the air, which shook the windows. But that one shook the solid hill so that the beams groaned. And after that the foreman came down from the quarry to tell her, with his hat still on his head, that her husband, who had been such a careful man always, had set too big a charge in the rock and used too short a fuse, and he'd blown himself and his mate Huw to pieces."

"I'm sorry," Davy had said. Then, after a long pause, because he was the sort of boy who likes to be sure about guesses, he had added, "What did the wife do?"

Granny had looked down at the flat silver ring on her finger.

"She married Davy's brother," she said. "Your Dadda."

2

Dadda

And now they were all quite different people . . .

Davy lay on the grass above the quarry cliff and tried to remember all he could about the three children who had first come to the farm on that strange extra holiday seven years ago.

Yes, quite different people. They had started changing almost at once. Perhaps it had been discovering that Mum couldn't be relied on either that had pulled them so close together, made them sentries of their own little fort, back to back, facing the world, relying only on each other.

They were still like that in a way, he thought. That hadn't changed. Even Ian, nineteen now, with his beard and his terrible old motor-bike and his odd friends from Cardiff University and his odder ones in Llangollen . . . He still made jokes, but they were bitter ones. He lived in a cloud of scorn, except for a few things such as the Welsh language and the Palestine guerrillas and the music of Berlioz. He never spoke to Dad if he could help it; he was polite to Mum and helpful with anything she wanted, but all without love.

Dadda and Granny were the people he loved. He was protective with Penny and Davy, but very silent, even on the long journeys when he drove them up to the farm in Dad's latest car.

Penny was different too, not just because she was fifteen and wore eye-shadow. He turned his head on the grass to look at her and found her looking at him.

"What's up?" she said, grinning.

"I was thinking about when we first came here and how different we all are now. Except Dad."

"Oh, Dad. Well, you can't expect . . . I don't know about Mum. I wonder what she'll come back with this time."

Davy laughed. Last time Mum had gone off on one of her "holidays" she'd got home with a black eye and two brand new suitcases, scarlet, with gold-plated clasps.

"Well, she's stopped doing it in term-time, for instance," he said.

"That's because she knows we can look after ourselves at home now. What she really enjoyed was upsetting the teachers by making us go away from school. Haven't you noticed how she hates teachers and loves mucking their arrangements about? I think it's because she still feels a bit guilty about not treating us right and so she resents anyone who might be treating us better."

"I expect that's it," said Davy. He was used now to Penny knowing so much about why people did what they did, and were like what they were like. He himself always found people quite mysterious. The gift seemed to make it harder for him to understand them, not easier. He had a fresh lesson in that fact almost at once.

"There goes another one," said Penny. "Hey!"

Davy looked along the cliff lip and saw a sheep poised as if it were making up its mind to dive into the abyss. At Penny's shout it did so, with a dainty little flounce.

"Idiot animals," said Penny, not moving.

"I expect it'll get out OK," said Davy.

Penny, walking up that way after breakfast, had found a sheep trapped on a tiny ledge about eight feet below the lip. It must have jumped down for the little strip of greener grass that grew there, and then been unable to jump back. She'd fetched Davy, and he'd climbed down to the ledge with a rope and a wide canvas belly-band, but the sheep had decided that he was some sort of dangerous predator and, driven by terror, had made a frantic, scrambling rush at the rock and somehow reached the top. Penny was still laughing when Davy reached the top, hot and nervy with height. He'd stopped swearing at her when he suddenly saw a large hawk spiral up from beyond the quarry, barely moving its wings but floating up like a glider on an invisible thermal. They'd lain side by side on the grass to watch it until it reached its altitude and sped north, straight and swift, as though it had a business appointment in Liverpool.

After that they'd simply lain there, drowsy with noon, making the most of the soft hill breeze.

"Gadarene sheep," said Penny, not moving but looking where this second idiot had disappeared.

Davy yawned.

"Do you suppose Dad . . ." he began.

"Let's leave him out," said Penny snappily.

"OK, OK."

He rolled on his back and tried to spot a lark that was tinkling somewhere in the blue. Already the cuckoos had stopped calling from hill to hill and were gone. In four more days he'd be back in Spenser Mills. In six the autumn term would have begun. But now . . . now if he lay here much longer he'd be asleep. He shut his eyes.

He saw a checked yellow oilcloth—the little table in Penny's bedroom at Spenser Mills. Her homework books in a pile. An open exercise book with a half-finished map of Australia showing. Her right hand picking up one of the black and orange pencils which Dad had brought home from his new job, very nice pencils with the firm's name in gold letters on the side. The hand moved as if to write, but stopped. Her left hand rose from the paper and gripped the point of the pencil. The right hand shifted its hold so that both thumbs pressed against the middle of the pencil. The finger knuckles whitened with strain. The wood snapped. He could not hear the clang as she dropped the pieces into her khaki metal wastepaper basket, but the picture was so solid that he could almost feel it.

"That was a waste," he said. He only spoke because he was off-guard and surprised.

"What was?"

"Breaking a new pencil like that."

Her face became stiff and white.

"How do you know?" she whispered.

Davy was frightened and ashamed. He'd long ago made a rule not to see any of his family's thoughts if he could help it. He had found he could drive them out by thinking hard about something else. But the picture had seemed so homely and harmless, and then had changed and made him inquisitive, and then the gift had worked this quick, small treachery.

"How did you know?" said Penny again, in more of a croak than a whisper.

He made her promise to keep the secret, then told her. Her cheeks were still white and her lips kept trying to moisten each other. She didn't look at him at all, and before he'd really finished she got up and walked stiffly along the top of the cliff. She stopped when she was about a hundred yards away and stood looking in the direction the hawk had flown, with the mild wind floating her hair sideways. He did not watch her long. Even at that distance he felt her need for privacy and turned his head away from the small figure outlined against the swelling mound of Moel Mawr. He was helping an ant find its path between grass-stems when he heard the rustle of her returning feet, and looked up. The wind and the warm sun had already dried the tear-streaks on her face.

"I'm sorry," he said. "I can't help it. It just happens."

"You're quite wrong!" she shouted. "I don't hate him! I love him! I love him !"

"I thought . . ."

"Well, you're wrong! He's a good man, sort of. Anyway, he's full of love. It's only the things he *does* . . . Those pencils . . . I know they're meant to be given away, so it wasn't even stealing. But . . . it was the *way* he did it, Davy, as if it were all something special for me, something he'd taken a lot of trouble over, something he expected me to love him back for . . ."

"All right," said Davy. "I suppose I like him. I don't think I love him, but . . ."

"But he hasn't got any friends," said Penny.

"He's got hundreds!"

"They aren't *friends*. They're . . . they're cronies. He knows everybody, he remembers all their names even if he hasn't seen them for years, they cheer up when they see him. But you don't feel that any of them would help him at all if he got into trouble."

"I suppose it's surprising he hasn't."

"What do you mean? He's *always* in trouble. Don't you remember when . . ."

There were a lot of whens to remember—contracts of employment not read—or that time three lorry loads of industrial filters had been promised to different customers when there was only half a load in existence—or the launderette where the economical home-made detergent seized up all the machines in one morning and turned the customers' clothes yellow—or . . .

"Real trouble," said Davy.

"Let's hope," she said. "You know, I think Spenser Mills is going to be different. I think he might settle down."

Davy shrugged. Penny settled cross-legged beside him and said in a voice which he could hear she was deliberately keeping calm, "Do you do it often?"

"See what you're thinking? No. I try not to, in fact. It happens, I can't make it happen. It's like weather, Granny said. Mostly when I'm tired or bored."

"OK. I see. Only don't tell me if it happens again. It's horrible—someone else knowing what you're thinking. It's like people coming into your room when you're not there, looking through all your drawers, reading all the bits of paper."

"I'm sorry. Anyway, I don't know what you're thinking—only what you're thinking *about*. You've got to be somebody who thinks in pictures to start with— Ian doesn't and Mum not much. And then . . . well, I know Dad and Granny quarrelled and Dadda tried to keep the peace. I've seen their faces, shouting. Dad used to be quite thin then. But I don't know what the quarrel was, or why it was so bad. I think it might have been something to do with the gift."

"I don't see why."

"Granny said it always brought grief—I expect that's right. I mean, look how you felt just now, when I let on. I expect it can be a lot worse than that, though."

"Grief? I was angry, but . . . yes, I suppose it could spoil things between us for ever—if we let it."

Davy said nothing.

"Grief's a funny word to use. Did Gran give you any for-instances?"

"There was another Davy . . ."

He stopped. It was Granny's very private story—he didn't think even Dadda knew. But there, at that moment, it seemed to him more important than anything not to let the gift break the trust and closeness that existed between Penny and him—so he went on with the whole story, trying to use the exact words Granny had used in the farm kitchen seven years before. When he'd finished Penny wriggled to the cliff edge and gazed down into the silent levels and screes.

"I wonder if it was true," she said.

"Of course it was."

"I mean she might only have been having a sort of fancy about being in love with Huw, but Davy thought it was real."

"It isn't like that. You can tell the difference. Look, you know old Mr Lydyard? He's the bloke at school I get a lot of pictures from—he makes History so dead boring that I'm always in the mood in his lessons. Sometimes when he's been writing on the blackboard he turns round and blinks at us as if he was surprised to see us there—and that's what it is. He's forgotten who he's teaching and thinks he's got a quite different class sitting there, one from before the war in another school, I expect. When he does that I can see what he's seeing, and it's so real I feel I could chuck the piece of chalk he's got in his hand and hit myself on the forehead. I don't get that with anyone else. I expect it's because he's a bit *gaga so* he has to *think* about what he's seeing, and I pick it up. Well, then there's times when he's thinking about something real which happened to him—he's got a favourite shot he once played at cricket, and there's another picture of a white road with trees down one side and goats tethered under the trees. I know they're real, like I knew about your pencil just now, but they don't feel as if they're happening to *me*. And then there's what you called fancies. For instance he thinks a lot about snogging with Mrs Oldbrow . . ."

"But he's *ancient!*"

"Poor old boy. Of course he's never done it. I know he hasn't because the pictures are all soft and they keep changing, like in dreams, and sometimes he gets her face wrong . . ."

"No wonder you're always getting C minus for history."

"I probably would anyway. I like now. But all I can tell you is Davy would have known if it was true, so . . . Oh, I don't like it, Penny. I'm afraid of it. Sometimes it's a bit interesting, but . . . oh, well, you're not the only one who thinks it's horrible."

"Cheer up. There's one good thing for you—I'm going to take care you're not bored when I'm about."

"Don't overdo it."

"I wonder why it's come to you. I wonder why it's there at all, just in our family."

"I don't know."

"Couldn't you ask Granny?"

"Well . . . she's never talked about it since that first time, but twice I've seen pictures of her remembering telling me. She was icing a chocolate cake, that day we had the singing party. It's funny. It's like seeing a photograph of yourself when you were almost a baby. I can remember everything she said, but I can't remember being me—what it was like, I mean. Anyway, I think she's sorry she told me all that—the thing is she wasn't sure whether she'd ever see me again, because she didn't know Mum would keep floating off. But I'm sure she doesn't want to talk about it now."

"Ask Dadda, then. It's his family. He'd know."

Davy made a reluctant grumbling noise.

"Please, Davy. Look, it's going to feel very . . . very *uncomfortable* for me from now on, knowing . . . I mean not knowing whether . . . I mean . . . Anyway, it won't be so bad if there's a reason—a beginning. Can't you see that?"

"Oh, all right. I'll try Dadda."

Summer ended while they were having tea. They came in from an afternoon so heavy with heat and the dust from seeded grasses that the air seemed almost as thick as water, so that you had to drag your limbs through it. Davy's ears popped with the change of pressure while he was waiting for the milk to boil for another cup of cocoa. By the time they were washing up the rain was thudding into the dust.

That first evening was glorious, with the heat and stickiness washed away and the dry hills drinking and moist odours filling their lungs. But then came three rainy days, when the cows came muddier each night from the hillside. Dadda kept eleven cows, a herd so mixed in origin that Ian said you could count thirty breeds among them—but they all got dirty. Penny was as fussy as a cat about wet weather, but Davy used to go and coax the animals home while Dadda started the generator and the vacuum pump and fetched the shiny churns from the milk-shed. Then together they cleaned the cows for milking. When he was younger Davy had felt squeamish about wiping down the sagging udders, but now he was used to it, and enjoyed the wet, half-sweet cow smell, and the stolid patience of the cows, and their large eyes and misty breath. His favourite was a black, squat, mischievous animal called Bella, who gave a lot of milk for her size and seemed to recognise Davy with a vague, cowish pleasure when he came from England.

There were six milking stalls, but only four buckets and four outlets from the vacuum pipe, which made for a complicated shift system. But the cows all knew their places and turns; when they'd eaten their cake and been milked and unchained they shambled back to the field without any orders. Davy fixed the sucking pipes to Bella and stood aside, watching their rhythmic jiggle as the pressure came and went, and listening to the thud of the generator and the rustle of rain on the slates.

"What's the best cow you've had, Dadda?" he said.

Dadda didn't often answer questions. Now he put his head on one side, frowned and shrugged; but Davy saw a picture of a broad, yellowish cow with a big bag and a bulging eye. He took his chance.

"She looks nice," he said carefully. "I'm glad you didn't have her de-horned."

Dadda tilted his head further still but he looked straight at Davy while his finger scratched at his cheek near the corner of his mouth. He hadn't shaved for two days, so his nail made a rasping sound on the upstroke.

"Before de-horning, she was," he said. "Yess, Gwenny told me you had our gift. And she's fond of you, Davy bach."

"I'm fond of her. We're lucky to have you."

Dadda scratched his spine and nodded, as though he agreed with the sentiment. But he said no more as he went to uncouple Nesta's bucket and pass it to Davy to carry through to the milk-shed. You were supposed for sanitary reasons to do this by going out into the yard and along the path there, but Dadda said, "Not likely, is it, the inspectors will come this weather?" So when it rained or snowed he always unlocked the old door which led direct to the milk-shed. Davy used this bucket to fill the first churn and started the cooler going.

"Do you know why we've got it, Dadda?" he said when he came back. "How it all started, I mean?"

Dadda scratched his cheek again and went on with the milking process. But when it was all finished and the buckets and pipes washed clean and the pump stopped (he let the generator run on to re-charge the batteries for that evening's lighting) he stopped at the door of the milk-shed, closed its lower half and leaned on it, looking out at the rainy evening. The cloud base lay against the hill-tops and sagged into the valley, drooping ragged patches which drifted slowly past, hiding and revealing the ranked, dark slopes of the Forestry Commission larches on the further hill.

"A poem there is," said Dadda. "All about Owain Glyn Dwr, you see? I could turn it to English."

"Please," said Davy. He'd never taken the trouble to learn more than the stammering of Welsh he needed to get through the hymns in Chapel. Ian was a fanatic for the language, and Davy thought one was enough in the family.

Now Dadda's voice deepened and his Welsh lilt became a half chant. At the end of each phrase he paused for several seconds, scratching his chin, while he ordered the next phrase into words that would do the Welsh justice.

By Maen Mynor stayed Glyn Dwr's standard.
Galaes his hawk gripped at his gauntlet.
Through the eyes of his hawk he viewed hill and valley.
He saw the Saxons scurry before his soldiers.
They were smoke blown sideways on the winter wind.
The smoke flies. It fades. So fled the Saxons.

The hands of the hillmen were red to the wrists.
By Maen Mynor stayed Glyn Dwr's standard.
And his captains came for praise and for profit.
"Hail to my harvesters," hollaed Glyn Dwr.
"Your swords were sickles to reap the red wheat.
But your purses are hungry. Soon shall they sup."

Last of the line bided Dafydd of Berwyn.
He kept many cattle in his close valley
And forty men had followed him to the mustering.
They had held the left flank by the Ford of Linan
Where the Saxons attacked with a sudden onset
Trusting by a trick to trap Glyn Dwr.
Without help they had held the ford all the forenoon.

"I do not ask praise. I do not ask profit.
I keep many cattle in my close valley.
Now all men know how I fought at the ford."

"You do not ask praise. You do not ask profit.
I must grant you a gift still, Dafydd the daring
So that men may not mutter I quarrel with my captains."

"I will not take land, nor loud-lowing cattle,
Nor gold, nor goods, nor a flock of fine fleece.
But grant me a gift such as you have, Glyn Dwr,
To see through the sight of the hawk on your hand."

By Maen Mynor a minute of stillness.
"Rash your request, but I cannot refuse it.

Privately shall you peep through the eyes of others.
And so shall your sons and their sons after,
Always wishing you had asked me more wisely.
They shall grieve for the gift through twenty generations,
The gift that is given for your fight at the ford,
The gift of Glyn Dwr. You cannot refuse it.
By a deed of like daring may your last son undo it."

Such was Glyn Dwr's answer to Dafydd.

When the poem was finished Dadda started scratching his chin again.

"Thank you," said Davy. "That makes three Davids. Is it something to do with the name?"

"You see," said Dadda, "it may not be true at all. The gift is in our family, so a man who was a poet would invent a poem, all lies, for the sake of explaining it, wouldn't he? I do not like to believe stories of that kind. They are not Christian."

"Yes . . . but some of it might be true. What about the battle? Where is Maen Mynor?"

"That means only Marble Rock. Anywhere it might be. But listen—in nineteen twenty-one a scholar from Oxford came to walk in these hills and stayed in our house. My brother Davy told him the poem—not saying anything about the gift, of course. And this scholar wrote later from Oxford, saying he could not discover any battle like that in any of the histories, nor a captain called Dafydd of Berwyn—but that would be a common enough name, wouldn't it, because these are the Berwyn Mountains."

"How long have we lived here?"

"We are in the parish registers for four hundred years, and perhaps we were here before that. Haven't you seen the silver ring Gwenny wears? The scholar was interested in that, too. He said it was a thousand years old. Our eldest sons have always given it to their wife at the wedding. Yes, your own mother is the first one not to wear it."

"I'm sorry. But when Ian marries . . . he's crazy about anything Welsh."

"You do not need to be crazy. Ian is a fine boy."

"Yes, of course. Have you got a copy of the poem, Dadda?"

Dadda didn't answer. But that evening he read the newspaper with less care than usual and kept his spectacles on when he had finished. Most evenings at this point he went round closing all the heavy oak shutters on the ground floor windows and making the lonely farm into a fortress against the dark. Then he would take Rud, his rangy, suspicious sheepdog, out for a last check that all was well with the animals. But tonight he sat where he was, with his old, scratched spectacles on his nose, until Rud rose from the hearth and came across to see what had caused this change of routine. Dadda scratched Rud's hackles, sighed, rose and hauled out from the dresser one of the cardboard shoe-boxes in which he kept the farm accounts and other papers. He scrabbled slowly through this one and at last brought out a single sheet which he handed to Davy.

"That is yours now," he said. "You must make yourself better at Welsh before you can read it."

The poem had been typed long ago on a big-lettered machine. The paper was yellow at the edges but white in the middle, which showed that it had seldom been looked at. Davy puzzled it through until bedtime with the help of Ian's dictionary and his memory of Dadda's English version. Then he lay in the dark, listening to the shuffling movements of the rain and its tinkle down the drainpipe by his window. The poem was fairly satisfying, even if it wasn't true. It was at least a way of thinking about the gift, a tool to handle it with, a lens that made it less mysterious by bringing it into focus. In fact it would be better if it wasn't true . . . twenty generations . . . a deed of like daring . . . twenty twenty-fives was five hundred. Penny had brought her history books to revise for O-levels, and had looked up Owen Glendower for Davy. About A.D. 1500. Add five hundred and that makes two thousand. And the first David, Dafydd of Berwyn, had been a grown man, so you could subtract twenty-five years . . . any time now . . . a deed of like daring . . .

I hope it's not true, he thought. I hope it isn't me. But I'd like to be rid of it. It's a nuisance. It frightens me.

3

Wolf

Early next term Davy was given a new lesson in the depths and dangers of his gift.

Spenser Mills was a New Town. It was so new that half of it wasn't even built yet. Only three years before nothing had stood among those close, ambling, south-midland fields except three dull little villages and the buildings of a dozen large farms. Now there were wide, well-lit roads, and curving rows of spruce new houses, and towers of flats, and brand new pubs and shops, and two industrial estates, so that in places you could bicycle along feeling that you were miles from the country. But then you'd swing round a corner and the road and lamp-posts would surge on in front of you but there'd be no houses at all—or, even more uncanny, neat rows of foundations with all the drain-pipes sticking into the air, but nothing else. Or you'd come to a churned acre of mud in the middle of which stood three bewildered elms, which had once towered above a hedgerow and now waited, carefully fenced against being bashed by cranes and bulldozers, to see how they were going to fit into the brisk townscape which was still only on the architects' drawings.

The Prices had come to Spenser Mills in the early spring. Dad hadn't had a job since Christmas but then, all of a sudden, he landed a very good post in the Labour Office of one of the huge contracting firms that were doing the actual building. The firm put them into one of its own new houses, which was empty because it didn't come quite up to what the firm called "Our own high standards of completion". This really meant that parts of the house were so badly built that if they'd sold it to some eager citizen he'd have been sure to complain and there might have been a public fuss with stories in the papers. But they knew their own employees wouldn't kick.

The chief trouble was that when it rained with the wind in the north-west the water somehow hummocked itself out of the gutter and came streaming down the wall of the best bedroom. And some joists must have been left out of the bathroom floor, because the bath had tried to sag through into the hall. The firm had kindly put this right by filling the hall with scaffolding, which meant that the front door wouldn't open and you had to edge sideways to get into the sitting-room, whose door—to even things up— wouldn't shut. And the gas central heating, if you turned it on at all, made all the radiators so hot that their paint stank.

It was these problems, rather than anything Dad had done, that had made Mum go off on the "holiday" from which she'd returned with the black eye and the red suitcases.

But things had improved when Penny and Davy got back to Spenser Mills. Dad had worked one of his wangles inside the firm, as a result of which three workmen who should have been bringing a different house up to "our own high standards of completion" had spent a week putting the roof right and propping up the bathroom joists more sensibly. He'd also managed to swap the boiler, so now the house was as good as any other in the road, provided nobody ran more than six inches of water into the bath.

Mum had changed, too. She'd managed to lay right off one sort of nerve pills and to cut down on two of the others. She had a bank account which she dared to use, and had joined a bridge club. She opened letters the day they came, reasonably sure now that none of them would be a threat from a debt-collecting agency. She stuck to the same hairstyle for several weeks at a time, and stopped badgering Penny about her own hair.

"In fact," said Penny, "I don't feel every time she comes into the room I'm going to be got at about something."

"It's great to hear her laugh," said Davy. "Have you noticed? She says something pretty silly and you laugh at her, she joins in and her laugh sounds clever, as though she knew all along?"

"I found her snogging with Dad in the kitchen last

night. She laughed so much she gave herself hiccups. So did Dad."

"I wondered what that noise was about. I suppose they don't think they're really as ancient as we think they are."

"Of course not. Dad's eased off a bit, too."

This was true, though you had to know him well to notice it. He sometimes spent whole evenings behaving like an ordinary, tired citizen and not like a compere at a ninth-rate beauty contest, as Ian had described it. (Ian was in Cardiff, which helped to ease the tension.) He had even bought a car which hardly rattled and didn't smell, a white Ford Corsair only two years old, of which he was immensely proud. He was longing to teach Penny to drive.

School, Davy thought, was OK too. The building stood about three-quarters of a mile from their house. It was a show place, a big new Comprehensive, and educationists and architects came from all over the world to study it. From the outside it looked as though its own architect would really have been happier designing forts and gun emplacements, because it was built of brutal grey concrete with many gaunt projections. Once you were in, though, you found that he must also have been mad about greenhouses— almost all the roof was glass, and on sunny days whole classes slowly roasted. Apart from that Davy liked it. The equipment was marvellous, the other kids OK, and the teachers a less dejected lot than he'd found at some of his other schools. If only Dad could stick to his job, he thought, he might get decent results when his O-levels came round in a year and a half.

In keeping with its architecture the school was always trying out new theories, and Davy's year was being given a real bashing at what the children called local geog. For the first half of the term they spent one whole morning every fortnight out in the town, or the country round about, finding out how the sudden rise in population had affected farmers, or counting and analysing the goods traffic through the station, or mapping the old silted canal, or drawing diagrams of the earth layers in some great hole which the builders had excavated. In the second half of the term they were going to split into pairs to study separate projects. And at the end of it all an educational researcher in London was going to analyse their work and write a thesis.

The second local geog expedition that term took them to the head offices of Dad's firm, which were in twenty caravans on a site which would one day be a pleasure ground. All morning they were talked to and shown maps and diagrams and plans by a smooth-faced man who called them "kiddies"; so, though it ought to have been interesting to know what was going to happen to the town next, the whole class was thoroughly bored and rebellious by the time they got back to the coach and found that the driver had disappeared.

It was a muggy, windless September morning. Davy

looked out of the window and tried to guess which caravan Dad was working in, but there was no way of knowing, so he lounged back in his seat, sleepy with heat and airlessness.

A picture floated into his mind. This very coach, fat and sleek by the kerb of the mud-streaked road, all its colours too bright to be true. It came nearer, and Davy hoped it was the driver returning, but then he saw that the picture was framed by the windscreen of a car, with a peacock-blue bonnet showing at the bottom, so whoever's thoughts he was picking up was sitting in a car. And the car was still now. There was something funny about the too-vivid colours of the coach and the bonnet. Davy was just about to crane round and see who was looking at the scene in that strange way when the picture shrugged itself. A line of little holes raced along the paintwork. The windows smashed. Orange flames and oily smoke billowed up. Children were rushing out of the coach door, screaming, but the same little lines of holes dotted to and fro over them and they fell in sprawled heaps on the road. Just as Davy noticed the barrel of the machine-gun juddering in the foreground the picture was all wiped clean.

But it was still a picture, a vague blank of fawny yellow, like perfectly smooth sand. Into this blank, from the furry darkness of its edge, wriggled a whirling black shape. It darted erratically about like a protozoon under a microscope. And now there was another, and another, and then more, all coming from different sides, smothering the smooth yellow in a whirling storm of black squiggles. They meant nothing, and that made them more horrible, worse than the picture of the blazing coach. Their mad, meaningless mess increased and increased its fury with a pounding rhythm, pumping yet more rage and terror into a mind that already seemed about to burst with the pressure of them. Davy was opening his mouth to yell when the horror was all suddenly wiped out, just as the coach had been, and there was the fawny blank again. Into the blank a squiggle darted, and then another . . .

The complete process, from blank to blank, lasted about ten seconds. It happened a dozen times and then there was the road again, and the coach and the mud-streaks, all looking as though they were lit with a strong sun. When the first line of bullet holes slashed across the paintwork Davy drove the picture from his mind with the seventeen times table and twisted round in his seat to look back along the road.

A car had appeared about forty yards back, a bright blue Jaguar, but not peacock blue. But if that was where the pictures were coming from you couldn't see the coach door from there. Whoever it was had *invented* a door and steps, and made them seem as real as the coach; and he'd done the same with the flames and the gun. It was as though he couldn't tell the difference. Only the sunlit colours were too garish for this dull day.

Davy cringed back into his seat, frightened and worried. It wasn't only the horribleness of the pictures or the madness of the mind that thought them. It was the way they never let up. He'd never felt anything like this before.

In the comfort of his seat he automatically relaxed— and there were the pictures again. The road, the coach, the mud . . . but on the far kerb a round figure was walking away with a well-known jaunty stride, in his shirt-sleeves with his jacket over his arm. Davy drove the pictures out, sat up and looked forward. Dad was there, in the real world, striding away just like that. In the picture he was twice riddled with bullets and fell screaming into the gutter, but in the real world he walked on unharmed. When he was getting small in the distance the blue car accelerated past the coach and the pictures faded.

Davy watched the car slow beside Dad, and saw him halt. The conversation only took a few seconds before Dad raised his arm as if he was acknowledging some remark. The car moved on. Dad stood at the kerb gazing after it, then turned and walked slowly back towards the caravans. The bounce had gone out of his step. He never noticed Davy.

Next week was September's finest. Davy wheeled his bike out of the garage and stood waiting for Penny, breathing deeply at the prickling sweet morning air.

"You'll be taking cold baths before breakfast soon," said Penny.

"It's almost as good as Wales," he said. "It's as though

it hadn't realised it was all town here now, and was still trying to be country."

Penny freewheeled out into the road without answering. He had to pedal hard to catch her.

"What's up?" he said.

"Didn't you notice? Dad? Last night?"

"Nothing special."

"Mr Observant!"

"Well, what?"

"Oh, he's done something. Or he's going to do something. He was all bounce and laughs. You must have noticed. Just like last time he got the sack."

"Oh Lord, I hope not."

"So do I. Hi, Charlotte!"

Davy fell back so that Penny could bike beside her fat friend and talk about diets, pop, and the amorous scandals of the Upper Fifth. The delicate, delicious air seemed stale now. He told himself that the blue car might only have stopped to ask Dad the way somewhere. But in that case, why had Dad turned back to the office, and with so depressed a walk?

"We'll be at The Painted Lady," said Mum.

"No we won't," said Dad. "I've gone off it. We'll be at the White Admiral."

The White Admiral was their usual Saturday pub, but this was Wednesday night and Mum had become sufficiently irritated by Dad's ceaseless jauntiness to insist that he should take her out somewhere. Now she stood in the hall and pouted down at her new white drill trouser suit with the bell-bottomed legs.

"I'm not going to the White Admiral in this," she grumbled. "I'll have to change again. Tommy Middle-ditch will go on and on. You know how he is."

Dad laughed and did a few steps of hornpipe in the tiny hall. They argued around and eventually settled to drive several miles to a village where there was a proper old pub, not named after a butterfly at all. Dad was pleased with the idea, as it meant a longer trip in his smart car.

"You'll be all right, darlings?" said Mum.

"I'm going to watch *Carry on Spying*," said Penny.

"You've seen it before," said Dad.

"Only eight times," said Penny. "It's that sort of film."

"Poor old Dave," said Dad.

"It's all right," said Davy. "I've got a lot of chemistry homework. I'll do it upstairs."

Davy liked to do homework on the floor, lying on his belly and writing with the paper only two inches from his nose. He wasn't short-sighted, but it made a change from school. Even so it was wearisome work. He was about half way through when the page blurred in front of his face and became a fawny yellow blank on to which a black squiggle darted, twirling with furious menace. Then another. Then another.

He shook his head, concentrated on the isotopes of

carbon and managed to force the idiot mess out of his mind. Even so he could still sense the pressure of it, like a shoulder against a door. Then the pressure relaxed and he did the same. Instantly he saw another picture. Night. A clear sky with a few stars. A house with lit windows. Only the stars were too big and bright and the windows glared as though there were a furnace inside. But the house was a particular house, the Prices' house, the one where Davy lay at that moment on the floor of his bedroom and Penny was watching *Carry on Spying* downstairs. So the man who had been in the blue car, who carried the furious squiggles in his mind, had not just been strolling past— he was standing somewhere out there in the dark, watching this house.

Without putting any more lights on Davy stole into the bathroom, shut the door and eased the curtains open. Under the pale glare of the street lamps the scene looked normal, all shades of grey and black. There was no one about.

Deliberately he relaxed and allowed a picture to form. It was the house again. The downstairs window shattered, then flared with an explosion. All the lights went out but a searchlight cut a white staring circle in the blackness, with the front door at its centre. Dad rushed out, shouting, and was gunned down. The same happened to a woman and two children, real people but not anybody Davy knew. Then the picture was wiped away and there was the fawny yellow blank, but before the whirling squiggles could rush in that too was wiped away, and the picture of the house came clear again, dark against the night sky with its two blazing windows. Davy tried not to bother with the explosion and the corpses, but to look where things like the gate and the lamp-posts were. Then he pushed the picture out of his mind again and studied the same things in the real world; he decided that whoever it was was standing further off than he had thought, in the shadow of the car-port of the empty house one down on the other side of the road. Quietly he went down and locked and bolted the back door and checked the downstairs windows. He couldn't do the lounge windows without making Penny ask questions, and Mum and Dad would want to come in through the front door.

While he was doing this he found that the pressure on his mind was much less at the back of the house, so he took his homework into Mum's room and finished it there, very quickly and badly.

After that he watched from the bathroom window for twenty minutes, but saw nothing outside his mind. Inside there were the same pictures over and over again, either the house being attacked or the furious squiggles. Only twice was there anything else: the first time it was a man in a boiler-suit huddled sideways on a muddy path, with a booted foot kicking fiercely at him. This had the clear feel of something that had actually happened and was now being remembered. The other thing was very vague and strange, a dark grey rounded mass, veined here and there with white. It looked, compared with everything else, cool and peaceful, but it seemed to have less meaning even than the squiggles.

Penny had switched off the TV.

"What was it?" said Davy.

"A documentary about Bolivia."

"What about the other channel?"

"Huh. This is do-you-good night. It's all about prisons."

"Oh Lord! I'll try that."

"In that case I'm going to bed."

"Not for a minute, Pen."

"I'm not going to sit up . . . Are you all right? You look awful."

"I'm all right."

"No you aren't. You'd better go to bed."

"When they come home. I'm not ill. It's . . ."

"Something to do with your gift?"

"Ung."

"I don't want to know then. But I'll sit up and hold your hand."

"Thanks."

The TV was a way of keeping the door of his mind shut, something to wedge against it so that the heavy shoulder outside could not thrust it open and flood him with hideous imaginings. He watched men sitting dully in cells, or moving dully down long corridors, or working dully in the workshops. Sometimes they chatted, or laughed, but there was a deadness about the way they moved. At first Davy thought that this was something to do with the pictures being filmed so that you never saw any of the prisoners' faces, but then he decided it was real. To be in prison was a sort of being dead.

"You don't really want to watch this," sighed Penny. "I'll play you racing demon. I'll have the pack that hasn't got the five of spades missing."

It wasn't quite such an effective wedge as TV, but it worked well enough till Mum and Dad came back, a little tight but in good tempers and very lovey-dovey. Davy watched Dad lock and bolt the door, and sighed with relief.

But when he went up to bed he found he could not begin to drowse without the pictures flooding through his mind again. He turned on his light and read *Greenmantle* for a while. Then he decided that the watcher might simply be waiting till the last light went out, so he switched it off, put on his jersey and trousers over his pyjamas, drew the curtains open and watched the street, standing well back from the window so that the street lamp would not reflect from his face. The pictures came more weakly and confusedly now, as though the watcher himself was sleepy, but the fragments Davy saw were much the same except that the woman who ran out of the house was now Mum.

After about twenty minutes the darkness under the car-port moved. Davy tensed for a dash to Mum's room, to shout to Dad that the house was being attacked; but the man who came down the driveway of the empty house swung off straight along the pavement. He was wearing a hat, so his face was in shadow; and the angle from the bedroom window made it hard to judge his height—about five foot six? Anyway, not tall. But big. Though his short overcoat was padded at the shoulders, even so Davy could see that he was really very broad across the back. The coat made him look like a soldier, and his hair seemed to be cut quite short too.

But there was one thing, even in that tricky light, that made Davy sure he would know the man again— he walked with a curious, springy, balanced step, as though he had an extra set of muscles in his legs which made him walk with that tense wariness, poised, like a tennis player waiting for the serve or a hunter in the jungle ready for the spring of the tiger. Watching that walk Davy decided that the man's name was Wolf. It would be easier to think about him if he had a name.

A minute later, well down the road, a car started. Its engine note muttered into the distance. Davy felt his way into bed, relishing the dreamless dark, and soon was deep asleep.

He didn't see Wolf again for more than a month.

It was rather a good month. Davy played regularly in the school Under Fifteen side; he joined a group of six boys who were making an SF film about the mice in the biology lab suddenly becoming super-intelligent; Ted Kauffman discovered an old BSA bike on a rubbish tip and Davy helped him drag it home and start trying to repair it. And at home Dad eased up a bit, back to what he'd been before the bad week when Wolf was about.

"I think it might be because he's actually doing a job he's quite good at," said Penny.

"He'd say that anyway—being good at it, I mean."

"I'm not talking about what he says. But he really is pretty clever about people. And this job seems to be mostly that—interviewing them, taking them on, sending them off to the places they're needed."

"At least he'd know all the dodges for interviews," said Davy. "He's flannelled his way through enough of his own."

"You've got to stop talking like that," said Penny seriously. "Stop thinking like that, even. I mean, we've got a chance of his being the sort of father other people have. We mustn't do anything to push him back to being old Dad."

"Buy Super New Dad," chanted Davy.

"With the miracle ingredient—*responsibility*," breathed Penny.

"Can *your* Dad tell right from wrong?" intoned Davy.

"No?" asked Penny.

"But Super New Dad can," they shouted together.

"Buy Super New Dad!"

One morning in Art Mr Locke showed Davy's class a lot of reproductions of abstracts by well-known painters and then told them to go and do likewise. The only rule was that there mustn't be anything in any of the pictures that could be recognised as a picture of something. Davy hated this sort of artwork. He was fairly good at drawing animals and houses and trees, though not so good with people; but he was hopeless if he didn't have something to work from. However he found a sheet of fawny yellow paper in the rack, pinned it to his board and with the side of a stick of charcoal scraped a furry darkness round the edges. Then he used the tip of the charcoal to dash a whirling squiggle into the middle of the sheet. And another. And another . . .

"I should stop there," said Mr Locke quietly over his shoulder. Davy had in fact decided that already. The mess was just at that point of pressure where you thought you would yell if it got any worse.

"That's pretty, uh, interesting," said Mr Locke. He was a tall thin man with bloodshot eyes and an orange beard that seemed to be all part of the tangle of his long orange hair. Penny said he washed it once a year. Now he stood swaying to and fro on his heels and looking at Davy's picture.

"Giving it, uh, a title?" he said in the mumbling voice he used when he was pleased with your work.

Davy moved away and looked at what he had done. It was not as bad as the real thing because the squiggles didn't dart about, but they looked as though they might.

"It's called 'Fury'," he said. "It's really a . . . a dream I once had—a sort of nightmare. The paper reminded me. I thought if I painted it it might help . . ."

"Uh," said Mr Locke, seeming to understand. "Don't take it off the board till you've fixed it or that charcoal will rub. I'll, uh, put it in one of the frames."

He did so, and hung it in the passage to Assembly, so that Davy had to pass it several times a day. He couldn't bear to look at it. The other children hardly noticed it, of course, but several of the teachers said it was disgusting and asked to have it moved. This only made Mr Locke like it even more, so that Davy (who usually only got "Shows interest and tries hard" on his art reports) won a prize with it at the end of term.

But that was weeks in the future now. By then the whole hideous adventure with Wolf, and Mr Black Hat, and Monkey, and Dad, seemed to be all over.

4

Ian

They had a bit of luck at half term. The school closed
for a week, and Dad had discovered a lorry driver who
spent his whole time taking loads of defective gas
boilers up to a factory in Birkenhead and bringing
fresh ones down. His route took him past Chester,
where he dropped Penny and Davy and arranged to
pick them up six days later. They caught a chugging
little single-coach train down the branch line to
Wrexham, where Dadda was waiting for them in the
same old car. It had been a cheap journey, but slow
and noisy and very tiring.

Davy slept too late next morning to help with the
milking, but he did his evening stint and thought that
Bella was pleased to see him, insofar as it is possible
to guess any of a cow's slow pleasures. He stood for a
while watching the pulse of her milk through the bit
of glass tube at the top of the bucket.

"I know that poem in Welsh, now," he said. "I know
it by heart."

Dadda said nothing, but smiled.

"Do you know anything about Glyn Dwr?" said

Davy. "I asked Mr Lydyard but he said it wasn't in the syllabus."

"Ach, it's too little history I remember. Glyn Dwr was the last Prince of all Wales, wasn't he? He beat the English many times, but they won in the end. He didn't die, though. Vanished he did. And he is in one of Shakespeare's plays—Henry the Fourth, isn't it?"

"I expect so," said Davy, not yet used to Dadda's habit of putting any statement he was quite sure of into the form of a question. He uncoupled the milk bucket, slapped Bella's tough flank and carried the bucket up to the milk-shed. It wasn't raining so he used the outside route, but when he got there he found that Dadda had unlocked the top half of the connecting door and was leaning on the bottom half.

"Glyn Dwr met a monk in the hills once," he murmured. "The monk looked him in the eye and said, 'Prince, you are born a hundred years before your hour.' Then he walked on, saying no more."

That didn't seem much help to anybody, Davy thought as he tilted Bella's milk into the churn.

"The hills are full of stories," said Dadda. "My Nain used to tell me them, about Arthur and Gawain and . . ."

"But they're all earlier. A thousand years earlier, Dadda. Henry the Fourth is fourteen hundred and something."

Dadda stroked his neck and thought about it.

"The stories will be truer then, won't they, bach?" he said. "You must ask Ian."

"Is he coming? I didn't know."

"He is a good boy," said Dadda. "He rides up here most Saturdays to fill himself with Gwenny's cooking, and sing in Chapel, and talk to his mad friends in Llangollen. Indeed he is late today."

"Oh, good. I haven't seen him for ages. Penny'll be glad, too."

As he spoke Rud dashed into the lane. His yelping drowned the deep burr of the bike as it took the steep inclines, and continued until Ian was actually standing there, straddled across the saddle, at the yard gate. The moment the engine cut Rud seemed to recognise who it was. Ian drew his left hand from his gauntlet and held it down for Rud to sniff; with his other hand he pushed his goggles back to show a savagely tired face.

"Hi, Davy," he said, grinning. "Good to see you. Penny here?"

He wheeled his bike into the yard and parked it under cover beside the old blue tractor just inside the gate.

That grin turned out to have been an effort at good-will. In fact Ian was snarly with exhaustion, having broken down on the journey and had to push his bike seven miles through Welsh hills till he'd come to a garage where he could repair his throttle link. He barely spoke to Penny and Davy while he ate a huge tea, and when that was over he immediately put on his leathers again.

"Where are you off to, for heaven's sake?" said Penny.

"Llangollen, ducky. See you tomorrow."

"Do you know anything about Owain Glyn Dwr?" said Davy, knowing it was a rotten moment.

"Look, I'm late, kid. And I'm not interested in historical codswallop. Look him up in the library."

"I've tried that. I can't find anything useful in the one at Spenser Mills."

"Typical English chauvinism. Anyway, I don't. Sorry. See you at breakfast."

"OK. I hope the bike behaves."

"It better had."

Penny and Davy waited despondently in the hallway until they heard the chuckle of the engine going easily down the hill.

"Has he got a girl in Llangollen?" said Penny as they went back into the kitchen.

"Ian has a girl in Cardiff," said Granny. "Black she is, but comely, like it says in the bible. From Nigeria, too. He has showed me her photograph."

"What's the hurry to get to Llangollen, then?" complained Penny.

"He is to meet his Nationalist friends," said Granny.

"Welsh Nationalists!" said Penny. "I thought they were a joke!"

"Silly they are sometimes," said Dadda, laying his papers on his lap, "but I do not think they are a joke."

"I thought they were private armies of six men who wanted to make everybody talk Welsh by law," said Penny.

"Yes, there are some like that," said Dadda. "A funny look in their eyes, they have, as though they expected the heavens to open and a troop of angels to come flying down, crying to the world in Welsh that the heaven on earth would begin on Thursday week."

"That'd puzzle the people who didn't understand Welsh," said Penny.

"Yes," said Dadda, and reached for his paper.

"But it is different with the water-boards," said Granny.

"Indeed it is," said Dadda. "Drowning good valleys to make a reservoir for Manchester. Whole farms have been lost, you see, where Welsh families have lived for ten generations. It is not a joke to try to stop behaviour of that sort."

"But what about the private armies and blowing up power stations?" said Penny. "That sounds pretty stupid."

"Yess," said Dadda. "But every time a Welshman does some little stupid thing, you must remember that a hundred Englishmen in London have done a hundred big stupid things. Look in the dresser, Davy bach. In the third box are some books. Isn't there a Shakespeare there?"

There was. Davy took it to bed with him and read carefully through *Henry the Fourth*, *Part I*. The pages were much more thumbed than those of any other play in the book.

Davy knew too much to try again at breakfast. He wasn't going to get much time with Ian, so it was stupid to waste it starting conversations that were only going to produce that rasping note of scorn. It's no fun to be hurt by people you're fond of. So it was a surprise when Ian looked up from his buttered eggs and said, "By the way, Dave, I found someone who can tell you about this Glyn Dwr bloke. I'll run you down after breakfast."

"After Chapel, you are saying," said Granny.

"Sure," said Ian. "Everything okey-doke with the deacons? I hope we get a couple of decent hymns."

They did. On the other hand the Minister had decided to prove that industrial pollution was the lesser beast in *The Book of Revelations,* Chapter Thirteen, verses eleven to eighteen. This took twenty-eight minutes by Penny's watch and was so dull that pictures kept swimming into Davy's mind, mostly thoughts that some of the men were having about Nancy Owen, the local beauty who had sung the solo anthem just before the sermon.

They have torn up the railway line that once ran from Llangollen westwards along the valley of the limpid Dee. Davy had been blinking forward over Ian's shoulder, his eyes full of tears from the rush of wind, so at first he thought he was looking at some sort of

bright bungalow at the bottom of the tilted lane down
from the main road to the railway. But when the tears
cleared he saw that it was indeed a railway carriage,
standing lonely on its siding, blazing with green and
gold paint and with its name, Morfudd, lettered
ornately on the side. It looked more like a gipsy
caravan than a railway coach. As they walked down the
steep timber steps towards it he saw that the
embankment on either side had been carefully
cultivated and was planted entirely with leeks.

By the time they reached the last step the door of
the coach was open and in the doorway stood a stout
little man wearing an old brown dressing-gown as if
it were a monk's habit; his beard and hair stood out
an equal distance all round his head; it was mostly grey
but tinged in places with an ugly yellow which might
have been its original colour but looked more likely
to be nicotine stains from the large curved pipe the
man was smoking. He took this from his mouth and
called a robust good morning in Welsh. Ian answered
him and introduced Davy in the same language.

"This is Doctor Huw Hughes-hughs," he said. "He
can tell you all you want to know about Glyn Dwr,
as well as all you don't."

The Doctor frowned fiercely at the sound
of English, but led the way into the coach. Most
of the interior partitions had been ripped out,
leaving a narrow, many-windowed room which
contained a bed and a cooker as well as ordinary
living-room furniture. Books covered much of the

floor in mounds and pyramids and tottering columns. Through the far windows Davy could see the Dee, brown and glassy, slide by. It was Sunday morning, so no one was fishing.

The Doctor turned to him with a snarl.

"Speaking no Welsh, indeed to goodness, and you wish to know of Glyn Dwr, whateffer?"

"Come off it, Huw," said Ian.

The Doctor laughed and spoke in ordinary English.

"Tell me how much you know," he said, "and I'll tell you the rest."

"We've only got an hour," said Ian. "Gran's got a leg in the oven."

He moved further up the coach, opened the padded lid of a bench-seat, took out some pieces of metal and settled down at the table where he started to rub them with fine emery paper.

"I know Glyn Dwr was the last Prince of all Wales," said Davy. "And I've read *Henry the Fourth*. But what I really want to know is something about a Welsh poem my Dadda taught me."

"I was under the impression your father had gone Saxon," said the Doctor.

"This was my grandfather. I'm afraid my accent isn't very good."

Nervously Davy repeated the strange, familiar lines.

"Your accent is better than that of many who think well of their own," said the Doctor. "That is an interesting fragment if it is genuine. I'll take a tape of it, if you don't mind."

He fetched a little cassette recorder, fiddled with the microphone and made Davy recite the poem again. Finally he played it back.

Davy watched Ian assemble three of his bits of metal into a vaguely familiar shape while he listened uneasily to a voice that he knew to be his own but sounded like a stranger's.

"Well," said the Doctor. "I expect you want to know whether it's a true story. Of course I can't tell you that."

"No, I know. But I thought you could tell me whether it *might* be true—I mean whether it sounds old enough, and whether there might have been a battle like that, and about Glyn Dwr's magic and things like that."

The Doctor listened once more to the tape, then nodded.

"Certainly it could be genuine," he said. "Most poetry of the period was more complicated than that, and about other themes. Your poem restricts its complexity to an elaborate pattern of alliteration, but there's no reason why it should not be genuine. Equally there is no reason why it should not be fake. It could, for instance, have been written somewhere in the eighteenth century, inspired by Macpherson's publication of his supposed Ossianic fragments, to account for a phenomenon of second sight running in one family. Is there such a thing in your family, Ian?"

"Not that I know of," said Ian, snapping his assembled bits of metal on to a tube so that it all became, instantly and obviously, the front end of a small machine-gun.

"This thing's going to blow like fury, Huw," he said. "But I don't think it'll jam any more."

Doctor Hughes-hughs rattled Welsh at him. Ian glanced at Davy, shook his head and laughed. Doctor Hughes-hughs sucked at his pipe, making the very bubbling of it sound doubtful.

"Why didn't you tell me about this poem earlier?" he said to Ian. "You know it's the sort of thing that interests me."

"Never heard it before," said Ian, not looking up from fastening butt to barrel. "Dadda didn't tell me, and if he had I wouldn't have bothered with it much. The trouble with our movement, Huw, is that there's too many of us dreaming about the past and not enough thinking about the future."

"They are all one," said Doctor Hughes-hughs smugly. "One continuing process. You and I, Dafydd, will explore the past glories of the Welsh struggle while your brother prepares for its coming ones."

He fetched books from various mounds, most of them in Welsh, and patiently translated bits about Glyn Dwr, and second sight, and the bardic tradition until Ian had completely assembled the gun. Davy found it hard to listen with proper attention while his brother loaded and unloaded several times, made a few adjustments, and finally took the thing apart and stored all the bits in separate little plastic bags, as though he were going to deep-freeze them. But the Doctor paid no more attention than if Ian had been doing the washing up.

At the top of the wooden steps Ian stood scowling back at the dark hills and the peaceful river and the gaudy coach. The cultivated plot on either side of the steps seemed especially to displease him.

"Leeks!" he muttered. "He doesn't even eat them— he grows them for the flower. What can you do with a movement full of that sort of joker?"

"Where did you get the gun?" whispered Davy.

"Huw bought it. We've got five. What are you going to do about that, huh?"

"Nothing. It's not my business. I mean . . . do you suppose you'd ever use it?"

Ian shrugged.

"Depends what you mean," he said. "We're using it now, in a way. Just the possibility of using it changes the situation. I want a free Wales—absolutely free, as separate from England as France is from Germany. Most of our idiot citizens would probably think I was a bit of a joke. But, for instance, if I took that gun and wrote 'Free Wales' in bullet holes across the front of the Town Hall they'd think I was a different kind of joke, huh?"

"I suppose so."

"Don't you worry, kid. The point is, we *are* a serious movement, and that means keeping the cowboys out."

He waved to the Doctor who had been watching them through a window that still bore its No Smoking notice, though his pipe was going like a chimney. The engine caught and revved, and they growled up to the main road.

In fact Davy did do something about the gun. He told Penny.

On the last day of every holiday they had always climbed to the top of Moel Mawr to repair the cairn that the three of them had built that first visit, and to add one more stone each. It was a sort of farewell to the hills. This time they had a poor day for it, with heavy masses of low cloud trundling slowly out of the west and the air so soggy with unfallen rain that all the other hills were hidden. The grasses up there were too coarse even for sheep, and now they were yellow and hissed thinly as they waited for the winter. The patches of bracken on the flanks of the hill were already darkening from gold to brown.

Penny and Ian both felt that they were really too old for this sort of ritual, and that it was sentimental of them to keep it up. But it was a good excuse for a walk, and it would have been just as sentimental, in a different way, to stop it. Still, Penny smiled awkwardly as she wedged a third stone into place.

"That's for Ian," she explained. "He began it. It was great to see him—he hasn't changed much, really."

"He's joined a group of Welsh Nationalists who've got machine-guns," said Davy, trying to make it sound like an ordinary little bit of news.

"Stupid nits," said Penny. "I've seen them on telly,

drilling and that. They're just like the kids in the Lower Third playing Normandy Invasion."

"Ian says he's serious."

"Like hell! What he's serious about is that England means Dad to him and Wales means something else— probably Mum, deep down. The book I read says all boys really want to bump their Dad off. Anyway, Ian can't put up with him any more."

"But if Dad's really going to settle down . . ."

"You can't tell. That might make it worse. Anyway, I'm not sure Dad is."

"Oh, forget it," said Davy. "We can't *do* anything about any of them—Dad or Ian—and it's too cold to stand around psychoanalysing our relations."

5

Mr Black Hat

Sonia Palozzi was a boisterous dark girl whose father was the steel erectors' foreman on the biggest new building site in Spenser Mills. At first Davy was irritated when he was paired off with her for the individual local geog projects for the second half of the term. The trouble was Sonia's love-life, which was very intense, but purely imaginary. She was always in a passion of ecstasy or despair, either for the new guitar teacher or for the drummer in some pop group, or perhaps a young policeman or a star footballer. Davy didn't want to have to listen to all that.

But then Sonia told him that her father said they could do the building-site as their project, go wherever they liked on it and ask any questions. Davy knew Mr Palozzi slightly, a serious, silent man who seemed to believe that the whole evolutionary process, from the amoebas through the dinosaurs and pithecanthropi, had been ordained solely in order to bring Sonia into existence. Dad, who worked for the same firm, said that Mr Palozzi was a sort of genius at his job. He spoke very little, perhaps because his English was erratic, but he could get his great metal spiderwebs into the air more quickly and safely than anybody else. If there was some snag in a job Mr Palozzi would spot it when everything was still on the ground; with other foremen snags show up when they've got a ton of girder swaying fifty feet in the air with the whole erection gang yelling and gesticulating from their perches. Mr Palozzi was a valuable bloke, Dad said.

On the first Friday after half term Davy met Sonia at the site entrance. Mr Palozzi with a referee's whistle clamped in his teeth came grinning over to lead them to a little hut where half a dozen men were drinking tea. He took the whistle out to explain as best he could that this was his daughter and she was a sacred object. One of the men winked at her. She turned as pink as a flamingo. Mr Palozzi looked murderously at the man and hustled her out of the hut.

Being a sacred object is difficult. For instance Mr Palozzi thought it quite improper that his daughter should climb ladders, so it was Davy who made his way up to a little platform on the girderwork while Sonia went off through the churned mud to measure and sketch the different strata of earth where the site had dug most deeply into the ground.

One day this was going to be the main shopping complex of Spenser Mills, but all Davy could see as he began his preliminary sketch was that the men and machines had dug a vast, rectangular wound in the clay; half of the wound had grown a scab of concrete, from which the web of girders was now rising; the other half was still hummocked mud, scored with crawler marks and littered with grids of reinforcing rods among which the blue glimmer of welding torches flared and vanished. A crawler crane was balancing a thin, immensely tall structure which dropped a grab twenty feet into the ground and brought it back carrying a quarter of a ton of clay which it dropped into a waiting spoil lorry. A dozen other machines were grumbling away in the mud, champing or heaving. It was all a busy mess.

Beyond the perimeter fence, running almost all round the site, was a circle of temporary buildings that housed the shops and banks that would one day find permanent homes in the complex. The places where they stood would then become a public garden and car park. Davy began to draw his aerial view of the site, thinking that it was going to make an interesting project and that he was lucky after all to have been paired with Sonia. He glanced across to the muddy end of the site to see how she was getting on.

A man was talking to her. She bit her pencil and then pointed back in Davy's direction. They started to pick their way back towards him, but before they reached the edge of the concrete Mr Palozzi met them. He started to wave his arms about, as if he couldn't argue well enough with words. Trouble, thought Davy, and climbed down the ladders.

Close under the girderwork a concrete lorry which had dumped its load was being hosed down by a workman who squirted the jet of water into the still turning drum to loosen the last of the load and prevent

...om caking on the return journey. The workman was Wolf.

Davy didn't realise this at once, though he might have guessed it from the picture he saw; the green of the lorry was too bright, its drum too round and fat, and the darkness inside it too thick and black; the sprayed droplets where the water battered the metal were far too brilliant for the weak sunlight of the real day. Davy pushed the picture out of his mind and looked directly at the man just in time to see the lorry driver walk over and say something. The workman scowled but handed his hose to the driver who rapidly sprayed down the chute and turned the water off. Davy relaxed.

Instantly the pictures came again—the driver huddled in the mud with a boot smashing into his face; the lorry bursting like a bomb; the first manic squiggle squirming across the sands.

"It's all right," said Sonia. Davy turned slowly and saw her at his elbow.

"What's all right?" he asked.

"Didn't you see? There was this bloke who came and said what was I doing and I told him and he said I couldn't because of safety so I took him to Pop and Pop's fixing him. You've got to come but it's going to be all right. He's gorgeous."

"Half a sec," said Davy. Wolf was still standing by the tap, watching his toy trundle away. That's what it was, a toy. His delight in washing it was a child's— there was even something childish about his hideous dreams. But he was a man, square, dark-browed, heavy jawed; you wouldn't have noticed him specially, though his nose was rather too small for his face. Suddenly his whole body twitched and he wandered away with the same springy step that Davy had seen before. His arms hardly swung at all as he walked, but his big hands clenched and unclenched by his hips.

"Sorry, kids," said the brown-eyed man in the office. His name was Mr Venn, and he was the site manager. "I can't have you scrambling all over the site, even if it is school work. It's not just that you'd get in the way of the job, but it's dead against safety regs."

"I am safe!" shouted Mr Palozzi. "When have I lost one man? You think I lose my own daughter?"

"OK, OK," said Mr Venn soothingly. "Nobody even busts a fingernail when you're on the job, Tony. But you know quite well head office wouldn't OK it, and if I took it on without asking them and then something *did* happen—or even if someone from head office just spotted them about the place—I'd get the sack. Sorry, Tony, I've got kids of my own. I'm not going to risk it."

"OK," said Mr Palozzi with sudden calmness. "I take my cards. I go home."

"Ah, come on, Tony," said Mr Venn, grinning at the threat. "I'll do anything I can for you, but . . ."

"You fix it," said Mr Palozzi.

"Well, look," said Mr Venn, "I don't mind them coming in here Friday mornings, provided they keep out of my way. They can see what's going on out of the window, or most of it. And if I go out on the site I'll try and take one of them with me."

"No good," said Mr Palozzi.

"Oh yes, Pop, *please,*" said Sonia. "That'll suit us fine."

Davy could tell from her voice what had happened. She had fallen in love with Mr Venn, who was just her type—quite young, cheerful, strong-looking, fresh-faced and only a little bit bald. Davy thought that working from the office was a good idea; it was warm and dry and soon November would be coming. And if the object of her love was actually in the room most of the time that would stop Sonia chattering about him. The main rule of Sonia's game was that her beloved should be the only person not to know what was happening.

"OK, OK," said Mr Palozzi, smiling. He picked up his hat, jammed his whistle between his teeth and left. Mr Venn sighed.

"I wouldn't do it for anyone else," he said.

The office was a hut in the air, six bleak little rooms perched on scaffolding just beside the second entrance to the site. It was outside the fence and a muddy pathway ran beneath it. Its large windows looked across the site to the other entrance, with the girder construction to the left and all the new churnings to the right. The other rooms were jammed with desks and filing-cabinets, but Mr Venn needed a bit of floor-space for conferences, so that Sonia and Davy found a nook between the filing cabinets and the window where they could see everything, not be in the way, and use the top of the cabinet as a writing surface.

From outside came the throb and clang of work; from inside the erratic jangle of several telephones and the ceaseless natter of code-like comment on the walkie-talkies with which the various foremen kept in touch. Mr Venn never seemed to have more than three minutes to work on any one problem before he was being harassed for a decision on something else—a consignment of castings three weeks late, a set of drawings that didn't marry up, a crane driver absent sick, a dispute between two trade unions, a message from head office saying that the chairman's wife wanted to choose the colour schemes, a complaint from the police about dirt lorries taking short cuts through residential streets, and so on. Even so he found time to come and ask how the project was going. Sonia sighed and blushed.

"Where do the workmen come from?" said Davy. "Do you know them all?"

"I try to. I have a word with anyone head office sends up."

"That's my Dad's job, I think," said Davy.

"I dare say. The only people who don't come from them are specialist drivers of really big plant. You hire the plant and the driver with it. But most of the blokes here were taken on at head office. They keep a pool of spare labour down there, so if any of their sites in town has a shortage they can supply it. I've just been talking to them about a crane driver I need—if they haven't got one they'll take him off one of the other sites if they have to. But he reports to me when he gets here, and after that I'm his boss for as long as I need him. You can only do it when you're running a really big show like we are in Spenser Mills—we've got over three thousand men scattered round the town. In twenty minutes you'll see the wages van start its round. That's quite a show—police car escort and everything."

His telephone rang, and at once he was deep in a complicated argument about copper piping. Davy made notes about what he'd been told before he forgot it, then looked out of the window to see if he could spot Wolf. Yes, there he was, unmistakable in his walk, carrying a shovel across the deep ruts where the concrete lorries ran, being shown something by a foreman, being shown it (to judge by impatient gestures) a second time, and at last bending to shovel a load of wet concrete into a hod; it looked as though the load had been dumped in the wrong place. Davy, at their house before last, had helped a neighbour lay a concrete path so he knew just how heavy the stuff was, but Wolf rammed his large shovel deep into the grey mass and lifted and tossed as though it weighed nothing; and then he wasted all the time his strength had gained him by taking several minutes to scrape up the last scattered remains of the pile. At last he leaned on the shovel and watched the winking light of a police car sliding past the entrance, followed by a dark security van, followed by another police car. Toys again, thought Davy.

Afternoon school ended at four. Davy waited for Penny at the gate and told her to tell Mum he wouldn't be home till six. He did forty minutes' maths homework in the library, then biked round to the site; opposite the main entrance was a stack of concrete storm drains on a patch between two temporary shops; a gang of five-year-olds were playing a bang-bang-you're dead game in and out of them. Davy chained his bike to a lamp-post and stood watching them with his back to the entrance. Wolf might go out the other way, of course. In that case he'd try again on Monday.

The hooter sounded. The clack and thud of machinery, which had already been dying away, stilled almost entirely. The new noise was the sound of homegoing, motorbikes starting, boots on tarmac, joshing farewells. Davy didn't even have to look round when Wolf came out: in his mind-picture an army tank was grinding through the crowd of men, mowing them down with its guns, crushing them under its tracks. Davy pushed all that from his mind, counted ten slowly and turned. A man with that distinctive, wild-animal walk was already moving down the far pavement by the site fencing. Davy let him pass the long queue at the bus stop, then followed on the other side of the road.

The pictures were still there when he chose to let

them come, though Davy was aware that if he'd fallen another twenty yards back they would have been too faint to register. Wolf seemed to be calmer now, seeing the street with almost ordinary eyes—but with colours still too garish, and with strangely squat buildings, and the lamp-posts and young saplings of what would one day be a tall avenue all impossibly thin and spindly. Once this picture vanished and Davy readied himself to drive away the frenzied squiggles that he thought were coming; but instead he saw that strange dark mass, marbled with snowy veins, that seemed to show that Wolf's raging mind was experiencing a moment of peace. Then this too vanished, and there was nothing.

Davy stopped and shook his head violently. He stared at the real street, of which for the last five minutes he'd only let himself be conscious enough to avoid walking into lamp-posts or stumbling over kerbs. Wolf was gone.

Obviously he had turned the corner by the fire station, a massive slab of building. Perhaps that had helped screen his thoughts. Davy would have liked to hurry, but he was frightened to. He could see Wolf's thoughts so clearly that he couldn't be sure that the gift didn't work both ways. Perhaps Wolf could see through Davy's eyes too. He might be just round the corner of the fire station, in ambush, waiting for a sign that would show that Davy had been deliberately following him. The only thing to do was stroll on . . .

Yes, Wolf was waiting, but not for Davy. The picture surged out before Davy reached the corner, a blue car standing empty at the kerb of the side street. Then a fury of squiggles, all rushing together in an instant, whirling and darting, going on and on, never being wiped away to show even a glimpse of the calm sands below. Davy winced and tried to push the horrors clear of his skull. He needed something to concentrate on. Ahead of him a dog was wetting a road sign, but at once it ran off under some bushes. A man was walking up the road on the other pavement, wearing a pale blue suit and a black hat. His shirt, tie, handkerchief, socks and shoes were all different shades of pale blue. His face was very brown, but not in a healthy way, pouched and flabby under the tan; and though he wasn't even middle-aged his body looked too heavy for his legs. He was clean shaven, but black sideburns came down in front of his ears right to the jawline. He was smoking a very long cigarette, and looked rich.

By the time he had painstakingly observed all these details Davy thought he had walked far enough to risk relaxing his defences, to see whether Wolf had mastered his frenzy. He had, but the new picture so startled Davy that he faltered in his stride and had to make an effort not to look over his shoulder. Wolf was back in this road, gazing this way; there was even a boy in the middle-distance of the picture walking along with a satchel at his hip. And in the foreground, blue as a kingfisher, came Wolf's hero, Wolf's God. Davy could feel the rush of joy and greeting and worship. But if it

had not been for the blue suit and the black hat he
would never have guessed that he was now seeing
through Wolf's eyes the man whom he'd studied so
carefully a minute before. Wolf's God was tall
and moved with lithe grace; his skin was as smooth
as a water-skier's in an airline ad. He was powerful
enough to own the universe and wise enough to
understand it.

And now he frowned. His lips spoke judgement.
Wolf cringed inside and turned away, shaking his
head, looking with misery down the side street
where he had been ordered to wait by his master's
empty car.

Davy walked on till the pictures were too faint to
catch. Poor Wolf, he thought. Poor Wolf.

"It's a funny thing," said Mum.

"I wish you wouldn't say that," said Penny. "It makes
me nervous. When you say something's funny it turns
out dead serious. But when you say it's serious you
give me hysterics."

"But I *am* serious," said Mum. "It *was* funny."

Penny made her burbling chortle and Mum smiled.
Davy was slightly jealous of Penny's knack of teasing
Mum just the right amount.

"What's funny?" he said.

"About being followed," said Mum.

Davy's knife faltered. He had a fetish of spreading
his peanut butter absolutely smooth across his toast.
Now he'd have to begin again.

"I expect you're used to it," said Penny placidly. "You're looking smashing these days."

"Oh, I'm always getting picked up," said Mum smugly. "Did I ever tell you about that parson . . ."

"Yes," said Penny. "What happened today?"

Mum looked at her reflection in a tea-spoon, frowned and put it down.

"Well, I was shopping and I went past Chepstow's— you know, the ironmonger—and I just stopped to look in the window . . ."

"What do *you* want in an ironmonger's?" fuffled Davy through his toast.

"Idiot," said Penny. "The window has a good reflection, of course."

"Yes it has," said Mum eagerly. "And that's how I saw this bloke."

"Tall and dashing, with a broken nose?" said Penny.

"He *did* have a broken nose," said Mum in a surprised voice. "But he was ever so little and his face was all wrinkled—I mean at first I thought it was a kid with one of those masks on, but then I saw it was just a bloke. He was standing a bit off, but I knew he was watching me."

"How?" said Davy.

"You get to know. *I* don't mind. Let 'em have a good look, if that's what they want. So I didn't think about it. But then, down in Market Row I spotted him again. I'd just come out of the butcher's and there he was on the other side of the street, him looking in a shop window this time, but he was still looking at me. And when I went up to Corinne's to see about my appointment, there he was again. And twice more after that, different places. But he was always keeping a bit off and pretending he wasn't there."

"Shy, I expect," said Penny. "If you don't like it you'll have to give up Corinne's and go to an ugly parlour, where they'll make you into an old hag, and then no one will bother you."

"No, it wasn't *like* that," insisted Mum. "I'll tell you what it was like. Do you remember that time in Bristol when your Dad got in a mess over those bananas and the police thought perhaps he'd been hijacking lorries or something, and anyway they followed me around for a week, to see what I was doing. I spotted them at once, of course, just like with this bloke. But there's no reason now . . ."

"Don't *champ,* Davy!" shouted Penny. "It's bad enough for Mum and me sitting here watching you wolf all those calories. You don't have to make that disgusting noise as well."

"You wouldn't have to worry if you'd take a bit of exercise," said Davy. "Football or something."

He meant it as a joke, but Penny threw herself into one of her rare fits of sulks. Mum, too, became irritable at hearing her little drama suddenly forgotten. And Dad was later than he should have been, and when he did get in he was exuding bounce and go. The evening soured. Mum declared a headache (like declaring war) and went early to bed. Penny lay brooding on the floor of her bedroom playing over and over again a Stones

LP which she knew everyone else in the house hated. Davy toiled through the rest of his homework, went out for a brief bike ride in the windy dark, and at last settled down with Dad in the lounge to watch a League Cup quarter-final on TV. It was a match to echo his mood, dull, rough, muddy and unskilful. He was almost asleep when he started picking up pictures from Dad.

Usually he would have shut them out at once, by working out the area of the TV screen in square centimetres and converting that to square inches, or something of the sort. But this particular evening had set its own mood on everything everybody did, a sort of distrust and dislike of each other, a self-concern and self-pity which made prying into Dad's mind seem, for the moment, a perfectly fair thing to do.

Anyway Dad's pictures never meant much, because they were day-dreams—Dad bringing off an impossible shot to win the Open Golf, with the tiny white ball soaring over a mighty tree to land within a foot of the pin at the eighteenth; Dad slamming forehand drives out of reach of a rattled Rod Laver; Dad scoring a couple of hundred runs against the clock in the final Test. Tonight, for instance, he was piloting a gleaming yacht across a sunlit bay; Penny was sunbathing on the deck by the cockpit and another figure—Ian, but without his beard—was marlin-fishing in the bows; a black steward in a white jacket appeared carrying a silver tray with a champagne bottle on it . . . and because it was that sort of evening

Davy's main feeling was not amusement but jealousy that he'd been left out of Dad's ridiculous dream of wealth.

And then the picture fogged and changed. This was something real, something whose solidity and dullness showed that it wasn't a day-dream but had really happened. A man in a pale blue suit with a matching shirt and tie was sitting at a table in a pub. Davy knew him at once. He was Wolf's God, Mr Black Hat. He pulled a leather wallet out and passed a five pound note to another man, who rose from the table and picked up some of the glasses. This second man was small, with a wrinkled face, but Davy couldn't see him well because Dad was concentrating on Mr Black Hat's wallet. It was very fat, and all the fatness was money.

One of the treacheries of the gift was that the moment you became interested in something it showed you the picture was snatched away. Now Davy's shock and worry broke in, and there was Dad lolling on the sofa, staring at the sweating footballers.

"That ref's blind," he said. "Did you ever see a foul like that?"

"I've been asleep," said Davy. "What's the score?"

"Nil nil. What a game!"

"I'm going to bed."

"So'm I, in a minute. Sleep well, old chap."

Davy paused outside Penny's door and listened. Mick Jagger was still telling the world, in a furious gargle, what it could do with itself. So there was no point in trying to talk to her now. It was going to be difficult, whenever he chose.

He chose Sunday morning. There was a ritual about week-ends. Dad washed and polished the car on Saturday afternoon (which he seemed to enjoy, though he'd never bothered with any of his other old bangers). On Sunday he put on a sporty blazer and took Mum to a pub, for the midday shouting match. Penny never got up till eleven, but then she washed her hair and got the dinner ready. It was always the same. Davy could be sure of finding her in the kitchen, with her hair rolled in a pink towel like a turban, peeling potatoes to roast with the ritual chicken.

"Can I help?" he said.

"You can lay the table, if you want to."

"I'll peel the spuds if you like, while you get your hair dry."

"What's come over you?"

"Well, I want to talk to you, and . . ."

"If it's about your gift, no thanks."

"It's important, Pen. It really is."

Penny levered an eye out of the white potato flesh with obsessive care.

"Is it about me?" she said.

"It's not about anything I've seen you thinking, if that's what you mean."

"Dad?"

"Yes."

"Hell! Oh, well, at least it might give me a

clue what's got into him. Hang on while I get the blower."

Davy took the peeler and set to work, sorting his thoughts out while Penny balanced the fan heater on the kitchen stool so that it was at a convenient height for her to sit with her dank locks in its warm blast. Then he told her what he knew, starting with the first awareness of Wolf at the caravan park, and going on to the night he felt him watching the house.

"I remember that," said Penny, shaking the first dry tresses out to float in the stream of air. "I knew you were dead scared about something. Go on."

By the time he'd finished all her hair was alive, electric with brushing, and her face was red with the heat from the fan. She went on brushing in silence.

"It means something," he said. "It all fits in, but I can't see how."

"Uh-huh. Don't be angry with me, Dave, but have you thought about it this way? Perhaps it's all coming from inside *you*. OK, I know you can do it—pick up people's thoughts—no, wait a sec—listen—I'm not getting at you, but can you tell the difference between someone else's pictures and pictures that you think of yourself and then persuade yourself they're coming from outside you? How do you *know*? You can't, can you? And this Wolf bloke—what you think are his thoughts are different anyway, so perhaps they really aren't his at all—no listen—you're sitting in the coach and you see this picture and of course you think it's coming from outside you so you attach it to the blokes

in the car. Next time you attach it to a bloke who was
doing something in that car-port, and he's got a funny
walk, and then you see him down at the site without
knowing you've seen him and that sets it off again.
Look, I'm not saying it *must* have. Only it *might* have."

Davy turned from the sink, cold all through. Penny
could be right and that would mean that he, Davy . . .
He forced himself to think properly.

"No," he said, sighing with relief. "It didn't happen
that way. That night I worked out where he was, by
the pictures, before I could see him. And he was there.
And when I followed him I saw the car in the pictures
before I saw it really, and it was the same car I'd seen
from the coach. I can't prove it, Pen. I mean I can't
prove it to *you*, I can only prove it to me."

"Fair enough. Dad's been jumpy as hell since half
term, specially those nights when he's late home.
Finished? OK, let's go."

She switched the blower off with a furious gesture,
snatched a saucepan up and shoved it down on the
gas.

"They won't be back for a couple of hours, nearly,"
said Davy.

"They can eat alone. I'm not waiting. What are you
going to do? Tackle Dad?"

"I can't. I promised Granny . . ."

"OK, OK, but you might have to, some day. Look,
I don't think you've got enough yet, anyway. Dad's
up to something, and it's connected with these
two blokes, and one of them watched our house

once and now he works on your site. And he's some kind of violent nut, too. And the other bloke's got a lot of money in his wallet. That's all we know."

"Dad couldn't stop thinking about that money."

"Yes, but that doesn't mean anything. You know Dad—he'd only have to see *anybody* flashing a lot of cash about to start day-dreaming. It's nothing to do with us. It's his look-out."

"If he gets involved with something that loses him his job, we'll be out of this house—out of Spenser Mills, probably. That's something to do with us."

"I suppose so. Only . . . only I don't see why *I* should get involved. Anyway you haven't got enough to go on yet. You'll just have to wait, and use that gift of yours. Be a spy."

"It's not like that," said Davy angrily. "It doesn't tell you anything you want to know—only just enough to make you worry or feel afraid."

"I bet real spies are like that," said Penny. "They don't find out much, and even that little bit might mean all sorts of things, and in the end the generals just guess."

"We can't just guess."

"I didn't say we could, stupid. But there's no harm in your sitting around with Dad a bit more, and trying to pick up pictures. Otherwise we'll just have to wait for something in the real world to happen."

Penny opened the freezer door and took out a packet of hamburgers which she savaged from their wrapping with a bread-knife. She slapped three down on the table, then paused with the fourth in mid air.

"That picture," she said. "The one they hung outside Assembly and there was that fuss about. Is that how your bloke thinks?"

"Some of the time," said Davy.

"Nasty," she said.

6

Monkey

The spy discovered nothing.

Davy took to doing his homework in the lounge, against the blah from the telly, instead of in his own room. All that happened was that he got worse marks and began to feel how tense and fragile a film was Dad's mask of confidence. Dad couldn't nowadays watch even his favourite programmes without switching channels every ten minutes, and when Mum insisted on seeing something right through he'd be out of his chair half the time, fiddling with the volume or the contrast or brightness controls. Davy lay behind the sofa with his books spread round him, trying to relax his mind and let the pictures come, but he saw nothing.

Only one night, in bed, in the dark, he heard Dad coming up the stairs, wheezing slightly with the climb. Or was he sighing? Anyway he was thinking about Granny. She sat in the sun by the larder door, shelling peas. She was young, and though she wasn't specially pretty Davy could understand now, for the first time, why that other Davy and his friend Huw had done what they had done. There was a shadow on the dark red tiles of the yard, the shadow of a boy watching his mother shell peas.

Davy didn't tell Penny about this. It was Dad's own private thing. He felt ashamed at having seen it himself.

Nothing else happened all that week and most of the next. November dragged away in cloud and drizzle until on the next local geog morning Davy picked his way to the building site along an unpaved path that sent reddish mud squelching up the sides of his shoes. It reminded him of Dad walking through the hoof-poached gateway of the farmyard. By the time he rounded the temporary bank the drizzle had thickened to real rain, and even when he reached the dark sheltered passage beneath the site office he had to dodge small waterfalls that had somehow made their way through.

Then Mr Venn's office was so warm and stuffy that you had to wipe the steam off the windows every time you wanted to look out at the site, where the workmen trudged through the cloying clay in yellow waterproofs. The job, like all building jobs, was behind schedule, but Mr Venn said that if the weather worsened he'd have to call the men in.

Mr Palozzi had ordered the digger crews (over whom he had no authority at all) to bring him anything interesting that the grabs came up with. So Davy was sketching a fossil sea-urchin when he heard a knock at the door and automatically looked round. All the time now, when he was on the site, he was afraid that he would come face to face with Wolf, that their eyes would meet, and that in that instant Wolf would know him as well as he knew Wolf.

But this was someone else, a little man with large eyes and a pale, wrinkled face. His nose had been broken. He looked amusing, but not quite human, in his enveloping waterproof. Davy knew him at once.

"What is it?" said Mr Venn.

"Sent up to drive your big digger, guvnor," said the man. "Lost your old driver, dincher?"

"That's right," said Mr Venn, making a tick on a list in front of him and then standing up to move a green peg on the complicated work-flow board behind his desk. "It's a Miller five-fifty. OK?"

"I druv a four-forty all last year, guv. I'll get the hang of it quick enough."

"Hell!" said Mr Venn, reaching for one of his telephones. "What are they playing at down there? They must have half-a-dozen five-fifty drivers in the pool."

"Sorry, guv. I was the only one. Donchew worry— aren't expecting to dig in this, are you? I'll have her doing conjuring tricks for you by the time this lets up."

He nodded towards the steamed windows, against which the rain was now thudding in a driving downpour. Mr Venn sighed and put the telephone down.

"OK," he said. "Give it a go. Your foreman's Mr Reynolds—blue hat, two white bands. He'll have the keys."

"Right, guv," said the man. "Hope you don't mind me asking, but what happened to the other bloke?"

"Uh?"

"The bloke who drove the digger before. I don't want to go the same way—learn by the mistakes of others, that's my mo'o."

There was something about the way he said this that sounded odd, almost teasing, to Davy; but Mr Venn only noticed the joky tone and laughed his big, easy laugh.

"Not much use to you," he said. "We had a bloody strong oaf of a labourer down there and somehow he managed to hit him on the leg with a shovel. Don't ask me how he did it, but he almost cut his foot off."

"OK, guv," said the man, laughing too. "I'll stay in my cab. So long."

Davy wiped the window for the tenth time and watched him cross the site; he passed a couple of drenched workmen but didn't stop to ask for directions. In fact he seemed to know his way already, making directly for one of the small huts near the opposite fence. He came out almost at once and ran to the big yellow excavator that had been standing idle all morning. His climb up to the cab was just as Davy would have expected, rapid as a monkey's despite the clinging waterproof.

Few of the other machines were running, so Davy

could hear the deep thud and knock as the big diesel started, and see how its cold cylinders puffed out foul smoke which the rain washed clean. After a longish pause the caterpillar tracks jerked in the mud; the excavator slurped back a couple of feet, stopped and slurped forward; its cab swung slowly from side to side; its long digging arm gestured this way and that. The man was only testing the controls, making sure he knew how to handle the machine; as he scooped at the weightless air the digger looked like a great gawky insect going through its clumsy mating dance in the rain.

"Well, that's something," said Mr Venn, who had been watching through the clear patch on Davy's window. "I can't tell just from that, of course. There's a lot of skill driving a digger like that—grabbing a full load out of the bottom of a twelve-foot trench each go, not wasting machine-hours by bringing it up in driblets. Blast this rain."

He went back to his desk, too busy to watch the Friday morning ritual of the security van hissing past with its police escort. Even on a morning like this, one or two shoppers stopped to see the procession, stirred, like Davy, by the mere notion of all that money. That would make Dad day-dream all right.

"Let's call him Monkey," said Penny. "That makes sense if the other one's called Wolf. You're sure it's the same man?"

Davy stuffed the sports pages of yesterday's *Sun* into

the toe of his left shoe and put both shoes, slippery with inner wetness, into the airing cupboard.

"I'm sure it's the man who was with Mr Black Hat when Dad saw his wallet. I'm pretty sure it's the same man who was watching Mum—you remember, she said he was little and he had a wrinkled face and a broken nose? But I can't be quite sure."

"OK. What's your theory?"

"He wanted the job driving the digger, I suppose, so he got Wolf to lay out the other driver with a shovel."

"Even so he couldn't be sure he'd get it."

"He could if Dad sent him up."

"Whatever for?"

"Money. Look, everybody wants jobs—they're always on about unemployment in the papers. Suppose Mr Black Hat is working a racket getting people jobs, taking a cut himself —I mean a week's wages off every bloke he places, something like that. If there isn't a job going he gets someone like Wolf to lay a bloke out, and then he gives Dad a cut to give the job to the right man."

Penny thought while she spooned Nescafé into her mug.

"Not enough money in it," she said.

"I don't know. Dad's isn't the only big firm in Spenser Mills. Suppose he's got a slightly bent bloke in all the other firms and they each get somebody a couple of jobs a week—that's about two hundred quid a week, say. Even if Dad and the others get half of it,

Black Hat finishes up with five thousand a year, tax free. Not bad."

"Yes, but . . ."

"Hold it!"

The back door rattled. A Martian staggered dripping into the kitchen.

"You oughtn't to put your head in a plastic bag, Mum," said Davy. "They're always warning you about that on the telly."

Mum raised trembling hands to the bag, then hesitated.

"How'm I going to get this off without it dripping on me?" she grumbled.

"Hang on. I'll dry it," said Davy, reaching for a tea-towel.

"No!" screamed Mum. "You'll push me out of shape!"

"OK, then, I'll roll it up from outside. That'll make a sort of gutter all round. I'll give you a penny for every drop that drips. Hold it. I'm going to stand on a chair."

"I left my new umbrella on the bus," complained Mum. "And then, coming back—I don't know where all the taxis go, Fridays."

They could tell from her tone that she had come home in a dodgy temper, but finding an audience waiting just inside the door was soothing her down. The plastic bag was opaque with rain, but close-to Davy could see that there was something of an unusual colour underneath it; he eased it off Mum's head as delicately as a girl in a flower-shop taking an orchid out of its cellophane.

Mum's hair was naturally nondescript, so the children were used to colour-changes: this time it was piled above her like a breaking wave and dyed pale pink.

"Oh, Mum, you are brave!" said Davy.

"Brave?" said Mum on a rising note.

"I think it's smashing," said Penny quickly. "What are you going to wear?"

This was the right question. Friday night was wages night, so the pubs were gay, and even families which got their money in monthly salaries, as Dad did now, dressed up to the nines.

"I thought I'd try that fawn outfit I got for Minorca," said Mum in jet-set tones, then added anxiously, "You really think it's all right? It was a new girl, an Australian, so I thought I'd give her a go, poor thing."

"The fawn'd be OK," said Penny. "Or what about your white suede? Why don't you go and try a few things out? I'll bring you up a cup of tea and judge the beauty contest."

"Lovely," said Mum, placid as a cow now. "Just help me off with my boots. I daren't bend down."

At last she padded out in her stockings, holding her neck very stiff as though her hair-do were a pitcher full of liquid which she was trying not to spill.

"Australians have a wicked sense of humour," whispered Davy.

"Shut up," said Penny. "D'you want another cup of coffee?"

"I suppose so. D'you think I'm right about Mr Black Hat?"

Penny watched the water run into the kettle as though it was important to fill it correctly to the nearest thousandth of an inch.

"No good," she said as she flicked the switch down. "There's too much doesn't fit. Wolf got sacked, didn't he? Dad's not flush enough with cash to be working a racket yet—and even he's not going to think he'll get rich enough to buy yachts your way."

"That mayn't be what the picture meant. You can't tell."

"OK, what about all this following Mum round, and watching the house? And Black Hat giving Monkey the money to buy drinks with, and making Wolf wait for him by his car—that's not how he'd go on if they were just, you know, *clients*. I mean, when he'd got them their jobs that'd be that. They're acting far more like they're all part of some *gang*."

"What for?"

"And Dad wouldn't be as jumpy as he is if he was only helping in that sort of racket. Is Mum on or off sugar?"

"Off, last I heard."

"I'll put some in and tell her I forgot. That'll keep her happy both ways. Are there enough men on your site for it to be worth their while pulling a wages snatch?"

"A hundred and forty-eight this week. Mr Venn says it'll be nearly eight hundred when the job's really going."

"How much do they take home?"

"He says a bit over forty quid a week, average."

"Six thousand quid—it sounds a lot, but it isn't really enough for a whole gang to be working on, is it? Or to buy yachts with."

"I suppose it might be the wages van," said Davy slowly. "That goes past, Fridays, taking wages to all the company's sites. It starts from the bank just behind our site, but it leaves us till the last, so I suppose it'd be pretty well empty by the time it got there. So there'd be no point in putting a couple of men on the site, and then letting one of them get sacked."

"How do you know it was only a couple?"

"I hadn't thought of that. What d'you think we ought to do?"

"Nothing," said Penny decisively. "If you aren't going to tell Dad about your gift, then we've got nothing to tackle him with—nothing that adds up, I mean. And even if we *knew*, I don't know it'd be any of our business—grassing on Dad to the police, or getting him to grass on his pals . . . Oh, he's such a fool! That's what bugs *me*!"

"You wouldn't rather he was a law-abiding citizen?"

"Course I would. But you've got to live with what you're landed with, haven't you?"

"I suppose so—unless you do an Ian."

"Look, Dave, all you can do is hang on and hope

for a fluke that'll tell you what's up. Then we'll know what to do."

"Let's just hope we're wrong about the whole thing. Your kettle's boiling."

"What d'you mean, *my* kettle? All right, all right, I'll make your coffee for you, my lord."

"You're pretty cool about it all, Pen."

She sighed as she watched the steam rise from the cups. "That's what you think," she said in a low, toneless voice. "I tell myself I've been brought up to live like the Japanese, in paper houses because of earthquakes—it's stupid to try for solid buildings. But I want to go on living here. Here. Going to the same school every term. Seeing Mum happy. Not having scribbles on my bedroom wall made by some other kid. I want to be somewhere where we belong—like Gran and Dadda do."

She looked through the swishing rain at the raw houses opposite.

"I'll give it four hundred years," she said. The mockery was a way of closing the lid on her feelings.

The fluke happened, but not in the way they'd hoped.

By Wednesday week Davy had the fidgets almost as badly as Dad. Term would soon be over, and that last week is always a restless time. And Dad's tense jauntiness was steadily growing more marked, worse than it had ever been, even at their most disastrous times, suggesting that whatever was going to happen was coming to its climax soon. Moreover Mum was getting ready for Christmas, which was always a difficult period for everyone else.

Mum had a fetish about Christmas. Everybody had to give the others proper presents, and they had all to be complete surprises when they were opened round the little twinkling tree at precisely ten a.m. The wrapping paper had to be a secret too—there had been one terrible year when Mum and Davy had both chosen the same pattern at Smiths, and another when Ian had insisted on wrapping his in newspaper. Even in their brokest years an extra quid or two had always crept into their pocket money by mid-December. Christmas, in Mum's view, was serious. In the children's view it was doom-laden. Mum was an appalling chooser of presents, always giving something too expensive that would suit the person she thought the recipient ought to be, rather than what that person actually was. And for months afterwards she would take note whether Penny was wearing her new jumper honourably often, and whether Ian (some years before) was using the chest-expander she'd found.

These pressures—from Dad and Mum and inside himself, though this was one of Dad's late evenings home—drove Davy out that Wednesday into a dry but muggy night. He told Mum he was going over to help Ted Kauffman with the BSA, but in fact he spent an hour simply biking round the whole network of new roads, sometimes dawdling, sometimes forcing his legs into an exasperated sprint. He rode in no special direction and at about seven o'clock found himself freewheeling down a curving avenue of slightly posher houses than their own. He knew where he was. This would bring him out on the main road opposite The Painted Lady, Dad's old pub which he'd now gone off.

The pub was floodlit on the outside, so Davy, thirty yards short of the junction, could quite clearly see the brisk little man who came to the door. It was Monkey.

Davy braked without thought, but Monkey was only peering up and down the main road, as though on the lookout for someone; then he turned and disappeared inside the bar. Davy swung his bike in behind a parked car, settled it against the kerb and knelt to fiddle with the adjustment of his dynamo. He was in the deeper shadow between the last two lamps of the side-street, and the pillar-box near the corner gave him some cover, but he could see the door of the pub.

In less than a minute it swung in; Monkey stood there again, jerking his head impatiently; four or five men jostled out behind him, hard to distinguish in the irregular light; the only clear thing was the turmoil of Wolf's violent images pulsing out across the dark. Davy shut them out by trying to study the other men.

One of them raised a cheery arm and accepted a slap on the back. Then he was strolling clear of the group and Davy could see that it was Dad. Two of the others moved off in the opposite direction, but Mr Black Hat and Wolf and Monkey stayed where they were. Mr Black Hat nodded down the road where Dad had gone and said something which made Monkey laugh.

Davy, half-relaxing now that Dad was out of sight, caught the picture that came at that moment from Wolf's mind—a long, drab corridor with a shiny floor, and a man in a sort of uniform walking along it with a leaden step and the despair of years on his shoulders. Davy had seen that sort of corridor, that sort of uniform, that sort of walk before, on the telly programme that night when Wolf had watched their house. The man was in prison, and he was Dad.

"It's up to you," said Penny. "If you think you've got to, then you've got to. I'm staying out of it."

7

Penny

Tuesday night was Mum's bridge class—the first real chance.

"Dad, I want to talk to you."

"Not now, old boy. I'm a bit fagged."

"It's serious, Dad."

"What's up. Trouble at school? Some of those young roughs . . ."

"It's about a man—I don't know his name—who wears a blue suit, blue everything in fact, and a black hat."

"I think I know the guy you mean," said Dad casually. "What about him?"

"There's another bloke—a little man with a pale face—and a big, strong, rather stupid bloke. I call them Monkey and Wolf."

"That's right. I've seen them a couple of times in the pub, with Trevor."

"Monkey's got a job at the new shopping centre site, and Wolf had one."

"Uh huh."

"Did you send them up there?"

"What the hell are you getting at?"

"They're friends of yours, aren't they, Dad?"

"What are you on about, lad? I'm not a snob—you know that. If I see a bloke at a pub who I've interviewed a week before, naturally I ask him how he's getting on. And if we both happen to use the same pub, of course we have a bit of a chat now and then. I'm damned if I'm going to go changing pubs because I've given one or two of the regulars their jobs."

He sounded quite angry about it, but otherwise not at all put out.

"You said you'd gone off The Painted Lady," said Davy.

Dad laughed.

"I'm not a snob," he said. "I didn't say Mum wasn't."

"Monkey only got that job," said Davy, "because Wolf broke the ankle of the man who drove the digger before. And Monkey didn't really know how to drive that particular digger. I was in Mr Venn's office, and he was pretty shifty about not getting a driver who knew the machine."

"Oh, for God's sake . . ." began Dad, then changed tack. "Why the hell do you call him Wolf? Dick's pretty dumb, but he wouldn't hurt a fly except by being clumsy."

This was it. Davy knew now that he wouldn't get anywhere by relying only on what he'd seen with his ordinary sight. It was true Dad had known the men in the Jaguar *before* Wolf and Monkey had got their jobs, but he'd probably have an answer to that. No wonder Penny had refused to help tackle him.

Davy thought of Granny. Perhaps she would never speak to him again, if he broke his promise. She would think of him as another Dad. That would be the sort of grief . . .

"Do you know anything about the gift, Dad?" he said. "The family gift?"

He needn't have added the last three words. Dad's face had already lost its flush and become grey-white, like something dead. And his hand had flashed to his chest and gripped there, over his heart. Davy waited, his own heart slamming, until a little colour had seeped back into those ghastly cheeks.

"The reason I call him Wolf," he said carefully, "is that there's something—two things—wrong with his mind. The first thing is that he thinks in horrible violent pictures all the time, shootings and smashings and burnings. The other thing is that I can see his pictures all the time, which I can't with anyone else. I don't know—perhaps there's some kind of pressure in his brain, a sort of bottle-neck, which makes him send out such strong pictures. Anyway, I call him Wolf because of what's in his mind and the way he walks. He's like that. A wolf—a mad one."

"He wouldn't hurt a fly," said Dad, but the thinness of his laugh showed that he'd only half recovered from his shock. "You should see him with Trevor—it's pathetic. He just sits there like a big sloppy puppy watching everything Trevor does as though it's one of the seven wonders of the world."

"That's the man I call Mr Black Hat," said Davy. "Yes, I've seen Wolf looking at him—he worships him. I suppose he's like one of those savage Alsatians that's only safe with its master. Wolf's been in prison, Dad. He knows what it's like."

Dad pulled himself together, as if he'd realised that he was on the edge of admitting more than he wanted to.

"Look here," he said in a kindly, fatherly, false voice, "this is all a lot of nonsense, Dave, and you're too old for it. I don't know who told you that silly old story, but they shouldn't have. There's no harm in a kid pretending he can see into other people's minds—I did it myself— but you ought to have grown out of that by now. It's bloody stupid playing detectives and snooping on your own Dad and making up stories about him, and I bet you a lot of other fathers would resent it like hell, that kind of story, shady deals. I don't resent that, Dave. But I'm not so struck on your persuading yourself it's all true. Have you been talking to Penny about this?"

Davy took a breath, slowly.

"A month ago, or a bit more," he said, "you were sitting in that chair having a day-dream about a yacht. Penny was sunbathing on the deck and Ian was fishing in the bows. A black steward brought you champagne. Then you started thinking about Mr Black Hat opening his wallet in a pub and giving Monkey cash to buy drinks with. Wait a sec. About a fortnight ago you were coming upstairs late at night and you were thinking about Granny shelling peas outside the larder

door in the sun, when you were a kid. I'm sorry. I
don't try and look in your mind, but sometimes it
happens by accident."

He waited. He knew he had very little more
ammunition. Dad's face had changed again, but it
wasn't shock this time. It was as though, for the
moment, he'd taken off the mask he had worn for
years and was now that other man he might have been,
weak, uncertain, longing to be loved.

"OK," he said, "OK. What about Penny?"

"She knows something's up. She understands about
people, much better than I do."

"Yeah," said Dad. "I've heard it's like that. It makes
you think you understand people, but you get them
wrong."

"I don't get Wolf wrong," said Davy.

Dad's mask slipped back on. It wasn't as though a
millimetre of the chubby flesh had shifted, but now
he was wearing it again.

"I wish you'd told me about this before," he said.
"There might be a lot of money in it—on the stage
and telly, you know."

Sometimes people say things so typical of themselves
that for a moment you think they must be mocking
you. It was like that now. Davy hesitated, then jerked
the conversation back to where it mattered.

"I haven't got Wolf wrong," he said again. "I know
how slippery the gift is. Of course I know. You don't
think I've had it so long that . . . Look, of course it
lets you down, of course it makes you think bad things

about people, of course it doesn't tell you all the truth, anything like. But Wolf's different. His mind's so simple and I can see it all the time. He got a job on the site. He watched this house one night. He broke a man's ankle so that Monkey could get a job driving the big digger. He's part of some business with you and Monkey and Mr Black Hat. I know all that, and I'm pretty certain it's against the law and they're going to ditch you at the end."

Dad's laugh was as confident as an ad for toothpaste.

"Don't you worry, boy," he said. "I can look after myself."

"Then I'm right?"

"You leave it to me. Things are going pretty well now. I've never had any luck in the past, but that's changing."

"We like living here, Dad, just as we are. Penny and Mum especially. We don't need anything else."

"Ach, it's good enough for a year or so, but I don't call it *living*—not compared with the things we could do if . . . Well, it's been great talking to you, Davy lad. Don't you worry. I've got it all under control. We'll sit tight for a bit and then push off and find an island somewhere and sunbathe and water-ski and eat great big steaks like a map of Europe."

There was no point in getting angry.

"Last Wednesday," said Davy slowly, "I was outside The Painted Lady—I didn't go there on purpose—I was just restless and biked around and fetched up there. Monkey came out first and checked that the street was

clear and then you all came out together, about six of
you. Monkey and Mr Black Hat and Wolf stayed by
the door and watched you walking away, and Mr Black
Hat said something which made Monkey laugh. But
Wolf made a picture of you. I saw it quite clearly—
you, in prison uniform, walking along a prison
corridor. He's been there, Dad. He knows what it's
like—I could see from the picture."

"That doesn't mean anything!"

"I don't know. If you add it on to all the other
things . . . Dad, I expect you're so used to people liking
you that you don't notice when they're only
pretending to."

"Rubbish!"

"How much do you know about them, Dad? I
mean, if they do ditch you have you got any sort of
hold on them, like being able to tell the police where
to find them? Because if you haven't, it'd *pay* them—
they wouldn't have to give you your share."

"I wish you'd trust me a bit more. They're dimwits,
I tell you. They haven't got a scrap of brain between
them, not counting Trevor."

Davy felt he'd made progress of a sort. Dad was at
least not bothering now to deny that he had some
connection with Mr Black Hat. He had slipped from
poo-poohing the idea to admitting it. But in some
ways the progress was worse than useless: Dad was
determined to go through with whatever the plot was,
and now Davy was in the know. Davy was trapped
into keeping the secret. Even if the plot was dangerous,

illegal, wicked, there was no question of Davy betraying his own father. He would have to wait, watch the thing happen and fail, watch the family fall apart, watch life become crippled again.

"Can't you back out?" he cried. "Please!"

"It's too late. I tell you it's too late!"

Dad's voice was angry and dismissive, but his eyes were anxious and his pose as he leaned forward in his chair was almost an appeal for help. But then it altered. His glance flicked over Davy's shoulder to the lounge door and with a tiny effort he became jaunty, jolly, competent old Dad.

"I've been listening at the kitchen hatch," whispered Penny. "I didn't want to but I had to. You've got to go to the police, Dad."

Dad shook his head.

"I've been thinking," said Davy. "I might be able to give Mr Venn a hint that something's up, and he could sack Monkey, and . . ."

"Shut up," said Penny. "It's got to be Dad or he'll be in just as much trouble as the others. It's the only hope."

"Can't be done," said Dad.

Penny walked over and looked down at him. She spoke in a flat voice like someone reciting a poem they've been made to learn and don't much care for.

"Listen," she said. "If you don't go to the police and tell them everything I'm not going to forgive you. I mean it. Not ever. Whether you get away with whatever you're planning or not. As soon as I'm old enough I'll go right away and forget you. I'll sponge you out of my mind, and you'll never see me again."

Yes, thought Davy, that's Penny's way—and Dad would know what it meant because he'd tried to do the same with Granny but he'd never been tough enough to forget. Penny was. And Penny was Dad's girl—she always had been. If she could make him see she meant it . . .

"You don't understand," whispered Dad.

"Then tell us," she said. "Just listening I got this much: you've set something up with these men and you think it's going to make you a lot of money, but if it goes wrong you'll be in prison for several years."

"A hundred and ninety thousand pounds," said Dad, almost as though the figures were a magical formula to give him new strength. "I get a sixth, and even if it goes wrong there's no reason why anyone should connect me with it. We can go on as we were— this house, your school, my job, but I'll have thirty-five thousand quid sitting in a bank in Switzerland."

It was typical of him to round the figure up, not down.

"What are you doing for your share?" asked Penny.

"I've done it. I've finished. They couldn't have begun without me. I got them jobs on that site next door to the bank. I stuck out for equal shares when all Trevor was offering was a mouldy couple of thou. But the beauty of it is I won't be anywhere near when they knock the bank over. I'll be sitting cosy in my caravan listening to the police sirens."

Penny laughed her disbelief.

"Davy's right," she said. "They're just using you. You don't really think they'll let you keep all that if you aren't taking any of the risk?"

"But he is," said Davy. "There's plenty to connect him. He got those men their jobs, and even Mr Venn noticed there was something funny about that. And anyway I'm sure they're planning to, er, shop him."

"Who are they?" said Penny. "Where do they come from?'

"I don't know. Don't look at me like that! It's not my fault, it's part of Trevor's system. The less we know about each other the better—I don't even know their surnames."

"But Mr Black Hat knows yours."

"Well, of course, he had to. It's all right, kids—Trev won't split."

Davy could see he no longer believed this. Perhaps he never really had, but now ugly-smelling bubbles of doubt were floating up through his mind.

"Well," said Penny, "what's their plan?"

"Knock the bank over, Friday before Christmas, catch the double wage packets."

"Yes, but how?"

"I don't *know!*" shouted Dad. They stared at him.

"That's Trev's system too," he muttered. "The less

we all know about each other's part, the less chance of information leaks. It makes sense."

"It makes sense as a way of keeping you in the dark," said Penny. "It shows they don't trust you. But even so, you know enough to tell the police, when it's going to happen, some of the men in it. You've got their names on file at the office, haven't you?"

"Not their real names . . . but look, kids, I don't like to tell you this, but I *can't* split to the cops. Trev's got me by the short hairs."

"What do you mean?" said Davy.

"Oh, hell . . . well, it wasn't really my fault, but you know I got that car a bit cheap? It was a couple of hundred quid below market price, so perhaps I ought to have guessed it was a stolen job. Wait a bit—I didn't *know* it was stolen, but I wasn't going to ask any questions. I mean . . . well . . . I got it from a friend of Trev's, anyway. So when Trev came up, smiling all over, a couple of weeks later and asked how the car was going, and let on that it was hot . . . well, then I practically was forced to go along with him, wasn't I?"

"No," said Penny.

"You don't understand," said Dad. "He'd only got to drop a line to the cops, anonymous, and they'd come and take it away. No compensation even if I managed to persuade 'em I never suspected. No car. Bang. We've got to have a car, haven't we?"

He made it sound as though he believed this to be a perfectly reasonable argument. Perhaps he did. After all it was the first car he'd ever owned that didn't rattle and smell.

"We can manage without a car," said Penny. "Mum doesn't drive and you only use it for going to the office and taking her out in the evening. But we can't manage without a house, and you and Mum at home, and you doing a job. Listen, Mum's got friends here—real friends, not just the people you talk to in the launderette. And I don't know if you know, but Mum's bloke—the one she goes off on her holidays with—he sent her a message a couple of weeks back saying what about Minorca, and this time she said no. And I'm getting friends, Dad, too—I've never had any before. We won't have that on your island, only other people who can never go home because of something they've done."

"What the hell do you know about it?" shouted Dad. Davy had seen that face before, seen it in Granny's mind, younger, shouting in her doorway.

"She didn't mean that, Dad," he said gently. "She wasn't talking about the farm."

Dad, half out of his chair, subsided and looked at Davy. His eyes said, "I'm trapped, I'm trapped. My son can see into my mind." He shook his head slowly.

"You've got it wrong," he said. "Things don't work that way. I mean, suppose I split, then maybe I can do a deal with the cops and stay out of the dock—but it'll all have to come out, what I've done, won't it? The firm's not going to like that. Bang goes my job. Bang goes this house. Bang goes school. We'll be back like we were before we came here."

He spoke with weariness, a man who had made a superhuman effort to clamber with his family on his back out of some hideous pit, and was now being cruelly pushed back into its depths.

"That's all right," said Penny. "It doesn't have to be *this* house. It doesn't have to be *that* job. You'll be OK—people like you—you'll find something. But I want us to stop running and running and settle down to being ordinary people, people who know who we are. I want us to belong in one place, that's what. And if you get caught in this—even if you don't get caught—we'll never have a chance. You'll run for the rest of your life, and I'll go away and find out who I am somewhere else. I've got to."

He shook his head again.

"Listen, Dad," whispered Penny, "I like you. I'll stick by you, whatever happens, whatever anyone else thinks. I mean that too."

The whisper was one of effort, but not of shame. Penny was a secret person, keeping her loves and fears and troubles shut away, never letting the world guess them. It must have been hard for her to say that, but she had done it. She had only one threat and one promise to make, to blot Dad out of her life or to go on loving him, so she had made them, direct and clear. That was Penny, too.

Dad stopped shaking his head and sat silent, gazing at the unlit bars of the electric fire.

"There's one thing," said Davy. "I've been bothered by the way Mr Black Hat let you all meet at The

Painted Lady like that. I'd have thought crooks kept separate, at least in public, when they'd got a job lined up. I wondered if he was keeping an eye on you, sort of, to see if you might be beginning to crack or slip. So if you go to the police now . . ."

Mysteriously, this challenge to Dad's powers of deception was what made up his mind for him. He chuckled.

"Don't you worry about that," he said. "You've got most of it right but you've got one thing wrong. These blokes aren't professionals. You say Dick's been in jail, but Trev's only a small-time operator who's managed to stay out of trouble. He's got away with a few little jobs and that's persuaded him he's some sort of Napoleon of Crime. He gets us down to The Painted Lady so as he can stand us a few drinks and flash his wallet around and be admired. He's always on about stop-watch timing and maps and diagrams and contingency plans, only he never lets on about details. Honestly, it's pathetic. He sits there puffing himself up and Dick watches him all the time like a dog and we say, 'Great, Trev, great.' I don't know why I got mixed up with him in the first place, except for the car. He's so self-absorbed that if you took a police whistle and blew it in his ear he wouldn't hardly notice."

This was a new Dad, bitchy and resentful. Perhaps he recognised Mr Black Hat as being the same type of dreamer as himself, and was jealous of how much closer he had come to making his dreams real.

"You've got to watch out for Wolf—I mean Dick,"

said Davy. "OK, he's pretty dumb, but he's dangerous. And if anything happens to Mr Black Hat . . ."

"Poor old Dick," said Dad.

"All right," said Penny. "When are you going?"

She made the question casual but inescapable.

"It's going to be a bit tricky," said Dad. "We've got the hell of a load of work down at the office, and . . ."

"Let's go now," said Penny. "Let's get it over."

Dad started on a dismissive laugh, but realised Penny's mood and became in an instant a decent citizen doing his public duty at considerable personal inconvenience, such as changing out of his bedroom slippers and getting the car out.

"You coming too?" he said. "I don't know how long this will take."

"Mum won't be back for a couple of hours," said Penny. "We'll drive down with you and bus back. We'll be OK."

She sounded as brisk and cheerful as a hospital nurse. Dad must have known she didn't trust him not to pass some pub on the way, drop off for a couple of drinks and change his mind. But it would have hurt his self-esteem to suggest it, and he was going to need all that. Penny cut him a couple of sandwiches. He hummed some old tune from "South Pacific" all the way down to the town centre.

Penny and Davy sat in silence on the bus until it dropped them at their stop in the gusty, moist night. There were few people about. Davy's left sole squeaked. The wind buffeted about but couldn't cause one ripple in the river of light where the street lamps wound between the houses.

"I might have guessed there was something dodgy about that car," said Penny.

"I never gave it a thought," said Davy. "It was just another thing that seemed to be going all right. D'you think he'll tell them everything?"

"He'll try not to, but they'll get it out of him. Oh, hell, why does he have to be so crazy? You know, I was thinking, when he's got us into a mess it's always been a crazy mess. I mean, he's not stupid, but some of the things he's done! It's as if he were doing it on purpose."

"He said he's never had any luck."

"What he *says* doesn't mean anything. Look, this time he's gone and got mixed up in something absolutely impossible—far crazier than ever before—it couldn't possibly have worked. D'you think it's just *because* we were getting settled and happy that he had to smash it all up? There are people like that, aren't there? They've got this yen to pull the roof down on themselves."

"I suppose so."

"But *why*?"

"I don't know. Sometimes I think it must all go back to his quarrel with Granny."

"You mean he wants to be there, really—and if he can't have that he doesn't want anything?"

"Something like that."

"So if we could find out what the quarrel was about . . ."

"I don't know. I bet the gift came into it somewhere, though."

"Don't you ever think about anything else?" snapped Penny. Davy didn't mind her crossness. He knew she must be absolutely drained by her effort with Dad.

"Did you see his face when I told him about having it?" he said.

"No. But I heard his voice. He went all Welsh for a bit."

"I didn't notice."

When they got home they made hot chocolate and went straight to bed, leaving a note for Mum on the kitchen table saying that Dad would be late home. Davy spent a restless night, waking and tossing and dozing his way through fuzzy, hurried dreams. He heard Dad get home at about three o'clock in the morning. A man's voice said good-night to him at the gate.

8

Mr Venn

Christmas fell on a Thursday. Term ended the Monday before. Most of the projects were finished, but Davy and Sonia had spun theirs out on purpose. For Sonia it meant one more morning in the company of beautiful Mr Venn. Her passion had lasted a record time, over six weeks, and for that last morning she brought her father's camera, pretending it was to take photographs for the project, but really in the hope that she'd be able to sneak a snapshot of her adored one.

Davy was glad to be there only because it would have been agony to be anywhere else. He was shivery with nerves. He couldn't stop sweating in spite of a morning so cold that the rutted mud round the site was a series of iron-hard ridges with white ice in the hollows; and then the steamy warmth inside the office made him sure that he was really going to be sick, instead of just feeling sick. Mr Venn had a bottle of whisky open on his desk and sent his wan little secretary out to buy cokes.

"You won't see much happening this morning, kids," he said. "Holiday slack-off beginning already.

Soon as they've got their wages, half my workforce
will be on the road for Dublin. Cheers."

Sonia blushed. Davy could see even her shins go
pinker under her tights. He drank a little festive coke,
which made him feel sicker than ever, and wiped the
window clean. He knew there'd be nothing to see this
side—the bank was behind the office and there was
no conceivable reason for asking Mr Venn to let him
spend the morning standing on the office stool and
peering through the tiny roof-level windows in that
wall. Sonia giggled beside him.

"Can you set this for me, Davy?" she whispered.
"Dad showed me how, but I couldn't listen."

Davy stared at the big blue lens with numbers and
symbols and little levers arranged round it in
concentric rings. Normally he'd have been able to
work it out, he thought, but not this morning. Not
this morning. He shook his head.

"Camera trouble?" said Mr Venn. "Bring it over and
I'll have a look. Ah, that's a nice job, Jap of course.
Lovely morning for it, too. You won't need anything
within thirty foot, so we'll set it for infinity. Eff sixteen
at a hundredth. Don't try and take anything at an angle
to the glass or you'll get a reflection. There. Now all
you've got to do is aim through this little window
here, hold it steady and press this knob. Make sure you
haven't got your fingers over the lens and wind on
each picture with this lever here. Got it?"

"Thank you ever so," said Sonia, who had been
listening to her heart's lord with her mouth open and

her mind shut, quite lost in adoration. As soon as they were back at the window she whispered, "You'll have to do it. I can't hold it still. I shiver when I look at him."

This gave Davy an excuse to wipe the window even more thoroughly. Outside, it was indeed a lovely morning for photography, more like January than December, the town glittering with frost and the clear sky pale as watercolour. The saplings in the far road had lost their leaves, and so had the two tall ash-trees that must once have been rooted in some hedgerow and now stood like lost giants among the raw new houses. But if there wasn't much green about there was plenty of other colour, with the fresh concrete of the foundations providing a background like pale canvas for the brilliant reds and yellows of the cranes and hoists and diggers and little dump-trucks, and the pinky orange of Mr Palozzi's network of girders. In fact it all looked almost as bright as one of the pictures Wolf saw in his mind; except that these colours were clearer, more wholesome, less menacing.

Davy raised the camera to his eye and swung it to and fro over the gaudy scene, telling himself that this was the perfect way of spying on the criminals without being seen staring at them. But in fact he was using the black, hard chunk of gadgetry as a screen between himself and the world; the prisms and lenses of the viewing aperture made the whole site tiny and distant, with the figures of the workmen unrecognisably small. One of them was climbing into the big digger—that

must be Monkey. Davy steadied the camera and clicked
the shutter to make sure he knew how; as he wound
on the film he saw Sonia frowning at him for having
wasted a frame on something that didn't include Mr
Venn.

He looked away from her in time to see the usual
two dark police cars and the black security van slide
past along the road and round the corner out of sight.
His heart began to thud. Sonia was writing. He stared
at Monkey's digger, thinking whatever it is, it's got to
be soon or the wages will be in that van. Minutes
dribbled away.

Suddenly a black puff rose from the digger's exhaust
and his heart bounced again at the sight. At first he
thought it was that inner shock that had caused the
windows to rattle; but then, for no reason, he
remembered Granny saying how the blasting at the
slate quarry used to shake the windows of the farm.
And the lights in the office had gone out and Mr Venn
had picked up one of his telephones and was saying,
"What the hell?" but not saying it into the mouthpiece.

Mr Venn slammed that telephone down, picked up
another and jiggled the cradle.

Mr Wribley—the pale, bothered man from the office
next door—poked his head into the room.

"My phones are dead, Mr Venn," he said.

"So are mine," said Mr Venn. "And the power's gone.
We've blown a bloody big fuse somewhere—didn't
you hear the thud?"

"Mr Venn . . ." began Davy.

"Not now, lad."

"That big digger's doing something funny," said Davy.

Mr Venn strolled irritably over, not believing it mattered. But his whole stance changed the moment he had wiped himself a mist-free patch with his hand and could see how Monkey's digger was, so to speak, elbowing its way towards the far entrance. The machine lurched and swayed. Its earth-scoop gesticulated like a clenched fist at the end of its arm. Its caterpillar tracks churned past a pile of reinforcing rods, catching the far ends so that the wicked iron whipped to and fro over the concrete.

"He's going across the air-lines!" yelled Mr Venn. "Get Reynolds on the intercom!"

But at that instant from Mr Wribley's office rose a steady, horrible electronic whoop.

"Radio's all jammed!" shouted Mr Wribley.

"Hell! Hell! Hell!" bellowed Mr Venn. He snatched up his white hard hat with a single red band across the top and rushed out of the office.

"Now!" shrieked Sonia above the hideous radio wail. "You can get him coming back!"

Mr Venn raced into sight down below, darting through the cluttered maze of building materials. Another man in a blue hat with two white bands was running from the far right. They were both going to be too late: Monkey's digger was already at the site entrance, its dangling arm poised. One of the crawler cranes, which Davy hadn't even noticed start, was chugging up behind it. A few workmen had gathered but were doing nothing except shout and gesticulate.

Out in the street a big lorry that seemed to have been waiting its turn to be filled with a load of spoil swung suddenly across the road just as the first police car came swirling round the corner. Davy had the camera already poised for Mr Venn's return, so he steadied on the scene at the gateway, snapped the shutter and wound the film on.

"Oh, oh, oh," shrieked Sonia, jumping up and down. The implacable whooping from the radio drowned all other noise.

The lorry had caught the police car full in the flank and it was lying on its side, a wreck, blocking the rest of the road. The security van braked violently and just managed not to collide with the wreckage. The second police car halted smartly, but all its occupants must have been staring at the chaos ahead; none of them noticed Monkey's digger trundle out of the gateway with a lurching rush. Its arm swung forward and caught the police car low in the flank just as the doors were opening; for an instant of juddering effort all stayed poised and then that police car was also on its side. Davy took another picture just as Monkey scrambled nimbly down from his still moving monster. He seemed to have left it running in low gear, for it was now trying to climb the wreckage of the police car with the trapped men inside.

The gateway was now clear for the crawler crane to barge out. Three men who had been hidden under sacks in the back of the spoil lorry jumped down and surrounded the security van. A policeman, obviously dazed, worked himself free from the wreck of the first car and staggered towards these men, shouting. He had blood all over his face. Davy took another picture just as one of the men turned and hit the policeman with a short club. The policeman dropped and lay still in the road. The man turned back as though he had simply swatted a fly and helped his comrades pass the big double chain that had been dangling from the hook of the crane under the chassis of the security van. They all four stood back. Monkey waved a hand. The crane jerked and staggered slightly as it took the weight of the van, swayed it into the air and dumped it bodily in the back of the spoil lorry.

The workmen at the gate were still shouting and gesticulating, but doing nothing about the theft of their wages. Suddenly Davy realised that the masked man who had been poised by the cab of the lorry, apparently doing nothing, in fact had a machine-gun in his hands.

Sonia screamed on and on, the intercom whooped, the office staff yelled and swore. Davy cut himself off from all this by taking pictures.

The van was in the lorry and the bandits were scrambling aboard when, up from the main road, flashed three more police cars. From somewhere out of sight on the other side a dozen policemen came running. Monkey, still in the road, yelled and pointed. The man with the gun swung round and pointed it

towards the policemen, who threw themselves flat on
their faces. There was too much noise in the office for
Davy to tell whether the man actually fired any shots,
but he remembered the camera in time to take another
picture as the man swung round and started to fire at
the police cars, shattering the windscreen of the
nearest. The other bandits were jumping from the lorry
and running in different directions. Two of them tried
to dash through the group of policemen who were
cautiously getting to their feet; both were collared.
Monkey and another man disappeared between the
Christmas-freckled shanty-shops beyond. The man
with the gun had his back to the lorry, so he never
noticed the door of the security van sliding forward
nor the black-helmeted security guard towering above
him. The long truncheon swung, and the gunman lay
sprawling by the big wheels. Davy by now was not
conscious of clicking the shutter and winding the film
on.

Another man who seemed to have been sitting in
the far side of the cab came running through the site
gates, straight at the crowd of workmen who still stood
dithering there. They scattered, leaving a single man in
his path. This man, instantly recognisable by the white
hard hat with the broad red band, crouched for a rugby
tackle, but the bandit jinked in his stride and swung
a slamming fist that caught Mr Venn below the ear and
dropped him like a log.

"Oh, oh, oh," shrieked Sonia and rushed from the
office.

The last bandit came straight on towards Davy, running as lightly and as neatly as a footballer. Like an onrushing wave his thoughts came before him: desperate, terrified images, hardly recognisable as the site because of the way all the things seen through those mad eyes seemed to crowd in, to lean, to reel, to steeple, to stand poised as masses of crushing weights about to fall out of the bitter sky. An elderly small workman ran across waving protesting arms, but in the picture he was hideous, squat and hungry, with teeth like a dog's. The blow that cut him down was an instant of savage joy; but then the office itself glowered, ready to fall like a trap, with white-faced monsters grinning at the windows. The gate was an iron ambush, the passage beneath the office a tunnel of terrors, and out beyond waited the furious houses.

Long after the last of Wolf's thoughts had faded into the distance Davy stood by the window, shaking his head, trying to free his mind of the memory of them. When he looked out again he saw that Sonia had reached Mr Venn and was kneeling by his body, cradling his head in her arms, watched by happy, excited, bewildered workmen. He took a picture of that scene, too. It was the end of the reel.

The whole raid, according to the newspapers, had taken four and a half minutes from start to finish.

There were three reasons why the newspapers, both on Saturday and Sunday, made so much of the story. First, nothing much else was happening by way of

news: no fresh wars, no arrested pop stars, no falling
governments, no footballers having tantrums, no air
disasters, no quins. Secondly Mr Black Hat's
Napoleonic planning excited the reporters, with its
bomb to put the site telephones out of order and its
jamming device to interrupt both the site and the
police-car radios. Besides that there were seven badly
injured policemen and one old workman still in a
coma; and the security guard who clobbered Mr Black
Hat from above turned out to have been the local golf
champion, so the headline writers had enjoyed
themselves with horrible sporting puns.

And thirdly there were Davy's photographs. Luck,
and the bright morning and the good lens had, even at
that range, produced a dozen beautiful pictures of the
whole action, about seven of them taken at the instant
when something thrilling was happening. Mr Wribley,
of all people, had first realised what Davy had done, and
had got in touch with his brother-in-law who was a
reporter on the local paper. This brother-in-law, a dour
and distrustful-sounding man called Mr Boland, had
firmly taken charge of the film; Davy, when he was
telling Penny and Mum about the adventure, forgot to
mention that he'd taken any photographs at all. (Dad
was down at the police station.)

It was a surprise, then, when Penny pushed the
paper across to him at breakfast and there was the
whole story again, frozen into separate instants—
Monkey leaping from the cab of the digger, the
policeman yelling with the blood on his face, Mr Black

Hat in his gangster's pose with the gun, Sonia crouched in the frozen lorry-tracks with Mr Venn's head in her lap. This last picture was for some reason especially dramatic; when Davy bicycled down the road and bought all the other papers he found that they'd almost all printed it, variously describing Sonia as a teen-age local beauty and an Italian tourist.

One Sunday paper carried an interview with Sonia, who seemed to have been unable to say anything except, "I love him. I love him. I love him," over and over again. Mr Palozzi was furious and began shouting about the honour of the family and sharpening an old bayonet he happened to have. (Mrs Venn was probably not specially pleased, either.) Luckily Mrs Palozzi, who was a plump Scot, thought the whole adventure extremely funny. Davy at once realised where Sonia had inherited her giggles from when Mrs Palozzi came up in her car on Sunday morning to ask Davy to come and explain to Mr Palozzi exactly what had been happening in the site office. Mr Palozzi had locked Sonia, weeping, in her bedroom, and was sitting by the kitchen table fingering the fine edge and point of his bayonet.

"It's all right, sir," said Davy, standing stiffly on the other side of the table. "Sonia's rather like that. She keeps falling in love and telling everyone about it except the person she's in love with. He never knows. Anyway it's usually a pop star or someone whose picture she's seen in a magazine, or someone on the telly."

He didn't say anything about the occasional schoolmaster in case Mr Palozzi started hanging about at the school gates with his bayonet.

"When I am young," muttered Mr Palozzi, "I have eight sisters. Eight. They sleep in one room, and in that room they have only one picture on the wall. One picture of the Holy Virgin. Right? Now I have one daughter, and she has on her wall not eight pictures— no—eighty. Eighty different men! I am disgusted!"

He threw his bayonet angrily into the bread-bin. Mrs Palozzi rumpled his close-cropped hair and laughed.

"There's safety in numbers, Tony," she said. "Come off it. Sonny's a good girl. You'll only put ideas into her head, playing the heavy Eyetie father like that."

"Playing!" snarled Mr Palozzi.

The doorbell rang. Mrs Palozzi bounced out into the hallway. Mr Palozzi looked at Davy and winked, but his frown returned at the sound of a man's voice interrupted by Mrs Palozzi's eager trills.

"Well, that's a weird thing," they heard her saying. "I've got the boy here too."

She led Mr Wribley's brother-in-law back into the kitchen.

"Palozzi," said Mr Palozzi, rising to shake hands.

"My name's Boland," said the brother-in-law. "I work for the *Examiner*."

"Pleased to meet you," lied Mr Palozzi.

"Hello, my lad," said Mr Boland. "You did all right with those pictures, didn't you? Beginner's luck!"

He sounded disgusted about it.

"It was Mr Palozzi's camera," explained Davy. "It's a smasher."

Mr Boland grunted.

"That's the trouble," he said. "Your mother told me you were down here, which is just as well. *I* don't know the legal position if X takes a lot of pics with Y's camera, and Z then sells them to half the world's press. So what I suggest is I take fifteen per cent commission and you split the rest. OK?"

"How much?" said Mr Palozzi sharply.

"Two hundred and twenty-three pounds eighty-two pence," said Mr Boland.

"Mama mia!" said Mr Palozzi.

"That leaves you ninety-five quid each," said Mr Boland. "OK?"

"I don't see we've any right to any of it," said Mrs Palozzi.

Mr Palozzi shrugged.

"I only happened to be holding the camera," said Davy. "Sonia could easily have taken all the pictures herself."

"If I know Sonny she was having hysterics on the floor," said Mrs Palozzi.

The argument circled round a couple of times and finally came home to roost on Mr Boland's original suggestion.

"OK," he said. "That's provided your parents agree, lad. I'll just drive you up there and settle it. I'll try and get you the money tomorrow, in time for a little extra Christmas shopping."

"No hurry, no hurry," said Mr Palozzi. "It all goes into Sonia's dowry."

"Does it just?" said Mrs Palozzi. "I'm taking fifteen per cent commission too."

Mr Palozzi slapped her plump buttock, grinning.

In the car, driving cautiously along the empty Sunday-morning streets, Mr Boland said, "Do you read the *Examiner*, lad?"

"Not very often, I'm afraid, sir."

"Don't apologise. The point is I do a piece every week called 'Personality Spot'. Usually it's about some local worthy, the new fire chief or a retiring headmaster, someone like that, as dull as ditchwater. I thought it might make a change to do you—Spenser Mills boy makes Fleet Street big time. What do you think?"

"I'm going to Wales on Tuesday," said Davy cautiously. "We go there every holidays to stay on our grandfather's farm."

"Lucky kids. It must make a change from all this," said Mr Boland. They had come over a slight rise and there lay half of Spenser Mills, new as a new toy in the winter brightness.

"Oh, yes," said Davy. "Our family have lived in that valley for four hundred years."

"Have they just? I can make something of that, too. The different way of life, and all that. Got any snaps of this farm?"

"I think Penny took some last hols. You'd do much better to interview her, sir. She's cleverer at putting things than I am."

"I'll do you both," said Mr Boland.

The interview went well. Mum and Dad were down at the pub, but Penny was cooking lunch, in a good mood, and voluble. They read the result in the crowded Christmas train going north, because Mr Boland had been thoughtful enough to come down to the station with a page proof of the paper. There, strange in the dark fresh ink, were photographs of the two of them "looking as though *we* were wanted by the police," Penny said, and one of her snapshots of the farm. Mr Boland was very hot on details. Everybody's exact ages and addresses were there.

"That'll amuse Granny, seeing her name in print," said Penny. "It's a pity there isn't a picture of Dad, though—I'd like her to see how he's changed."

"They've been very careful about leaving him out—all the papers. Haven't you noticed? I expect the police told them to."

"Well it's all over now," said Penny. "I think Dad might even keep his job—they can't fire the father of a local hero, can they? And the police have got everybody except your friend Wolf."

Dave looked out of the window, not really hearing the whine of the rails nor seeing the flat fields slithering backwards. He thought about Wolf, the least important member of the gang, Mr Black Hat's dog.

He remembered the whirling nightmare of images that had swept past the site-office, and how the whole world seemed to loom and tower to crush the running man. He forgot Mr Venn, stunned on the frozen ruts. He forgot the little old workman who had run across waving his arms and was now lying in the intensive care unit of the hospital.

"Poor Wolf," he muttered. "I hope he gets away."

9

Dad

Granny was different, changed even since half term. It wasn't anything obvious, but even on the first evening Davy realised that her movements had become slower; she had always been deliberate, but now she moved as though she were afraid of hurting herself. The pink and white of her cheeks had separated into distinct patches, and her little mouth, though it still could not smile, was no longer firm.

Next morning, Christmas Eve, Davy came in from the cowshed and found her stirring the porridge for breakfast, which was just what he would have expected. You kicked your boots off in the back porch, drew a big breath of crisp air (the tops of the hills were streaked with the first light snow), walked in your socks into the warm, cooking-smelling kitchen and there would be Granny stirring the porridge. Always.

And so she was that morning—only there was something wrong about her stance, about the position of her right arm. Silent in his socks Davy stole across and saw that she was having trouble holding the spoon;

she was clutching it with a curious, awkward grasp,
with her fourth and fifth fingers inside the handle.

"I'll do that," he said.

"It is my work," she answered, but she didn't resist
when he took the spoon from her.

"Have you hurt your hand?" he asked.

She sat down in Dadda's chair, which was something
he'd never seen her do before. Even Rud, stretched
beneath the table, gave a little puzzled growl.

"I had a fall in the yard, a month ago," she said.

"Did you trip?"

"No I did not, nor slip. I was walking from the shed
with some potatoes in my apron, and it was a dry
morning, and then I woke up on the parlour sofa
where Dadda and Ian had carried me. Oh, but I was
bruised. I lay in bed four days—me!—the doctor tried
to keep me there a week but I would not heed him.
The bruises have gone, and the stiffness, but these two
fingers, look, I cannot move them. A great hindrance
it is."

"What does the doctor say?"

"Oh, I am becoming old, so I must be careful. Do
not talk to Dadda about this, Davy, for it frets him.
He is saying we must sell the farm and go to live in
a little bungalow in Llangollen—and that would kill
him. Stir that pot now, before it burns."

Davy was glad to do so. In the flurry and mess of
their lives in England the farm had seemed fixed and
certain, a point of rest—not just because it was a solid
house that had stood through the centuries, but

because of the people who lived in it, Granny and
Dadda, acting and speaking for a life that was rooted
and continuing, like a great sycamore. Now it was as
though Davy had knocked on the trunk and heard it
boom hollow.

"I'm sorry," he said.

"Ach, don't you fret either. I have many good years
in me yet."

Davy decided that the porridge was hot enough so
he drew it off the plate and moved the kettle across.

"Gran," he said suddenly, "may I talk to you about
Dad?"

"You may try," she said drily.

"You remember about the gift I've got?" he said.

"Do not trust it, Davy. You cannot trust it."

"Yes, I know. I try not to let it even happen,
especially when I'm with the family. I let on to Penny
last holidays, but that was by mistake. But Dad . . . he's
always thinking about you, especially when he's tired
and unhappy."

"Do not trust it, Davy. Do not say one word, do
one deed, because of what your gift shows you. It has
been no friend to your family."

"I know—but I don't think it's quite like that. It's
dangerous because you can't help believing it's told
you more than it really has. It makes you think that
you know what other people are really like inside, but
you don't. Penny understands people much better than
I do. Shall I tell you what she says about Dad?"

"When is that girl going to get out of bed?"

"Half past eleven, probably. It's the first day of the hols."

"Worse than that Ian, isn't she? Help yourself then, and put the pot in the bottom of the oven."

Very carefully Davy spooned golden granules of sugar over the grey mess in his bowl to make an even, exact layer. He watched the cream, poured in at the edge, seeping through the gold. This childhood ritual still gave him inexplicable pleasure. Maliciously Granny waited until his mouth was full.

"Well, what does the girl say of him?" she snapped.

"Oh," spluttered Davy, swallowing so fast that he burnt his throat, "well, I don't know if you know, but Dad's always getting into difficulties and scrapes. We've lived in dozens of houses and flats, and three times in caravans, because he kept losing his jobs, usually for something . . . well, not nicking money out of the till, or anything like that . . . not quite . . . sometimes for making a mess of things . . . but he's good at some jobs—anything to do with people—and then it's been for something absolutely stupid. Oh, he'd settle in and Mum would find us a house and a school, and in a couple of months Dad would come home and say he'd been promoted and everything seemed to be going fine, and then . . . well, once he borrowed his boss's Rover without asking and drove it into a brick wall . . . things like that. And look, this last time we all thought everything was OK. We'd been at Spenser Mills for nearly a year and it felt as though we were going to stay there for good, and then Dad got himself stuck in something really stupid, far worse than ever before. I found out and Penny bullied him into putting things straight before it was too late. Well, because of that Penny and I talked about him a lot, and she says that when things start going OK he destroys them on purpose—subconscious on purpose, I mean—because that's not what he *really* wants. He wants to be here, at the farm, and if he can't have that he doesn't want anything. Do you see what I mean?"

"It was his choice. With his eyes open, too, he made it."

"But he isn't like that. I don't think anyone is, really. You never do anything just for one reason, and some of your reasons are open-eye ones, and some of them are too dark to see."

"Well?"

"Oh . . . I suppose what I wanted to say was couldn't you ask him and Mum to come and stay? If he could come here when he wanted, then he might stop always smashing things up, and . . ."

"It was his choice. It is still his choice."

"But it affects us all! Couldn't you just ask him?"

"It is for him to ask. He must ask my pardon."

Davy could think of nothing useful to say, so he ate porridge.

"It is not right that you should judge me," said Granny in a metallic voice. "You do not know what happened . . . ach, Davy, it is so long ago. Perhaps I will tell you, and then you will stop judging me. Well, it is to do with your gift still. Your father is not Dadda's

son, you know—he is the son of my Davy. He was
born seven months after the explosion at the quarry,
and before then the story was all up and down the
valley—not the true story, you see, but bits and pieces
that came to much the same thing. Think what it was
like, Davy, to go to the Chapel all in black for your
dead man and big with his child in you, and to be
preached at there for your wickedness. Ach, it is long
ago. Dadda was a good man, and he was lead tenor in
the choir, too. I think the Deacons valued him more
for his singing than his goodness—but all the same,
after that sermon he spoke to them and the Minister,
spoke to them strongly; but they shut their minds and
ears to him, so . . . well, after the explosion I had gone
back to my own home, though my own mother would
not speak to me, and Dadda came down there in his
Sunday coat and asked me to be his wife and live at
this farm again. I told him, of course, what Davy had
seen with his gift, but . . . ach, Dadda is a beautiful
soul. I will not tell you what he said.

"So your father was born in this house and grew
up as our son, laughing about the fields like my own
Davy. I was careful of him—watchful—too much,
perhaps. It is difficult when you have only the one.
There was an impatience in him, yes, he took that
from me . . . and then he was clever at school—not
scholarship clever but good enough for us to think of
sending him to college, which we would have had to
pay for then—not like now, it wasn't, with Ian getting
his education for nothing and yet so ungrateful—but

your father wanted to leave school as soon as he was allowed. He wanted to be a man, but we made him stay on, fretting to be away . . . not sulking, mind you, that was not his nature . . . ach, so many friends he had, there was never a boy like it. Often it was like living in one of your towns. He seemed to whistle them out of the bare hills to loiter around our door, leaning on their bicycles. Or he'd be off with them all Saturday down the town.

"Now I should have told you that we'd explained to him about the gift, telling it like it was a fairy story and not true at all. And when he was eight or nine he would pretend that he possessed it, for a game, though he did not. And then he forgot it. But now he and these other boys wanted a bit of money for one of their schemes, so they got up an entertainment in a youth hall down the town, singing and jokes, you know? And what does he do for his part? A mind-reading performance. To this day I do not know how he arranged it, but it was with a friend and they invented hidden signals, so the friend could walk among the audience and they gave him watches or letters or photographs, while your father stood blindfold on the stage and told them what his friend held in his hand. No harm in that, was there?"

Davy shook his head, though he knew Dad and could half guess what kind of thing was coming. Granny's voice had dropped to a soft rustle of syllables while she looked down at her right hand with its last two fingers bent inwards like the claws of a bird.

"It was Mrs Thomas from Llyndaes, never a friend of mine, walked up special to tell me. Tuesday morning it was, so I was baking and answered the door with flour to my elbows. My own son, she said, to make his silly little performance more amusing, had told all those people about the gift, and had told them also about me and my Davy and Huw. He pretended, of course, that it was a story about his great-granny, but there was enough of them to remember the explosion and to inform the others. Ach, I thanked Mrs Thomas and went back to my kitchen and finished my bread, and I remember thinking that it could never rise, not after news of that kind—but it rose, just as though nothing had happened. And angry I was, so that I could hardly explain to Dadda—but he coaxed it out of me, and then he coaxed me into forgiving the boy. Which I tried to, for Dadda's sake, but . . . but the way he answered. I had to say *something* to him, didn't I? I could not have let it lie, just like that. Oh, what he said to me, and what he said to Dadda when he came in from milking! How I'd killed two men and how I'd sucked the will out of a third and how I was trying to do the same to him, and how Dadda was a drudge and a coward to let me treat him so, and . . . ach, such stupid words to remember all these years . . .

"And then . . . well, he did not go away that day, nor that year, not walking out of the house I mean. But that was when I lost him. And when there were arguments after, ordinary arguments, there was always that underneath. Those nights I would lie awake and see, as clear as I see you, Mrs Thomas smirking on my doorstep and I'd feel the sticky flour all up my arms. And the arguments grew more bitter, and came more often, until . . . yes, he was after us to spend the money we'd put by, Dadda and I. He said the farm was too small for him, and he wanted to take in more of the hill for fields, and buy more animals, and build a big barn, all modern. But we did not want the change or the risk, we wanted to go on living quietly until we should die quietly. So then it came round to all that about how I had murdered his father, and I grew so angry that I said he must go—I do not remember the words I said, only my throat all tired, and me running to the door at last to try to stop him, and him shouting again at me and walking down the hill. And after that, why, of course Dadda was my husband and we had no children. There are many couples live like that."

She sounded very tired now, dried out with the effort of recalling that old sorrow. Her voice had no sap in it, her eyes were closed and the good fingers of her right hand turned and turned the flat silver ring on her left, unconscious of what they were doing.

"It does not sound very much," she said suddenly. "But to think of him standing there on that platform, telling my story to all those people, just to get a few shillings for my shame."

"Penny says he's a good man," said Davy. "She's the one who gets angriest with him, but I think that's because she understands him best and loves him most."

"I have never told you, but you are the image of

him. It's a knife in my side sometimes to see you stand in a doorway, and say something and laugh, with your head held just his fashion."

Davy didn't like the idea.

"I'm *not* him," he said. "I can't imagine me doing what he did, or some of the other things he's done to Mum and us. But . . . you know, Dad isn't what he *does.* All that's just something that happens to him on the surface, but inside . . . you know you sometimes see the moon on a windy night with the clouds racing over it and it looks as though it's the moon that's rushing along when really it's standing still—he's like that."

"He has only to ask my pardon and he will be welcome here."

"Couldn't you start it off—write him a letter? Please, Granny."

"The new eggs are in the yellow crock."

"Aren't there any of yesterday's?"

"Look in the blue one, then."

And of course Granny would know exactly how many eggs had been left from yesterday, just as she'd know that Davy had enough sense to prefer them. It was her way of saying neither yes or no.

Perhaps she wrote. It didn't matter, except to her and Dad.

Penny was listening to Radio One next afternoon and caught a familiar word in the news bulletin. She came rushing down the steep home field to where Dadda and Ian and Davy were repairing the lambing pens, ready for the year's first lambs which always seemed to be born just as the worst storms of January set in. This was bitter work, standing still in the nagging wind and tying poles and hurdles into position. You can't knock a nail in properly, nor lash cord firm, if you are wearing gloves, so Davy had no feeling at all in his fingers when he heard Rud's intelligent little yap, that meant something of interest was happening. In the next instant he heard Penny's shout, too, and saw her careering down the slope. He was glad of the excuse to straighten up and search for warmth with his hands in his trouser pockets. Penny started gabbling before she reached them.

"It was on the wireless! There's been a bomb in our house!"

Dadda and Ian stopped work too.

"I'm sure it must be ours," she panted. "It said Spenser Mills and a key witness in the bank raid case."

"Where was Mum?" said Ian.

"They're both OK. Miraculous escape, it said. It went off at ten o'clock this morning. The house was wrecked. But there was no one in it. Attempted murder, the police say. They think the timing device went wrong, otherwise . . ."

"He wouldn't have understood it," muttered Davy.
'Who?"

"Wolf. Mr Black Hat had time bombs. He used them to blow up the site generators."

"What the hell are you on about?" said Ian. Davy shrugged and looked at Penny.

"Ian," said Dadda, "wouldn't you like to get on your bicycle and ride down to Mr Prichard's. He will let you use his telephone and then you could try to find out what has happened, couldn't you?"

It was almost an order, which was why he made it sound like a question. Ian jerked his head at Davy, telling him to come too. Together they plodded up the field.

"Now," said Ian, as soon as they were out of earshot, "what's he been up to this time?"

"Oh, you know that bit in the newspaper about me and Penny and the photographs I took . . ."

"Didn't bother to read it. Nothing to do with me."

"Well . . . Look, there isn't time . . ."

Ian scowled, but indeed they were nearly at the farm and it was an understood rule that they didn't talk about Dad when Granny might overhear. Ian got into his leathers, Davy put on two extra layers of clothing, the bike started first kick.

Ian went carefully down the lane. Even in midwinter you couldn't be sure that some idiot tourist wouldn't come dicing up the slope with his family lurching around in the back seat as he took the tight bends. Davy clutched hard at his brother's waist, leaning into the corners as he'd been taught; perhaps he'd been too numbed with cold down at the lambing pens, but now the shock of news, if it was true, chilled him from the inside as much as the whistling air did from the outside. When he had hoped that Wolf would escape he had never thought of him coming back for revenge, or to prevent Dad from going into the witness box. Wolf would do *anything* if he believed, in the turmoil of his mind, that it would help Mr Black Hat.

Suddenly Ian pulled in to one of the little widenings which had been made to allow cars to pass in the narrow lane. He switched the engine off and said, "OK. Fire ahead."

"Well," said Davy, "those photographs you didn't look at, the reason why I was there at all that morning was . . ."

He had been half thinking of concealing from Ian that Dad had been at any stage an accomplice. After all, he might easily have stumbled on the plot somehow. But Davy didn't like the idea of not trusting Ian completely, so he told him the whole story, leaving out only the existence of the gift. Ian wouldn't understand about that. Trying to tell the story fast he made a mess of getting events in their right order. When he finished Ian laughed.

"You've got to hand it to him," he said. "Dad's consistent, if nothing else. So now he's lost the house after all. What about his job?"

"Penny says if he really wants to keep it he'll manage somehow. I wish he could be friends with Granny again."

"It probably wasn't all his fault," said Ian surprisingly. "Gran's a dear old biddy, but she's a moral thug as well. I don't think she's ever given way over anything."

"Don't you remember, the first time we came, I twisted my ankle in the quarry and she wanted Dadda to whip Penny and you said you'd never forgive her if he did? You shouted at her, and Dadda made her change her mind."

"Lord, that was long ago. I'd completely forgotten that. OK, let's get on."

He kicked the starter, but the half-warm engine was temperamental and he was still kicking when a glossy dark car rounded the lower bend and drummed powerfully up the hill; by the lamp on its roof, though it wasn't flashing, they could see it was a police car. As it whisked past the bay where they were waiting Davy saw a face in the rear window and a hand waving, but the car was gone before he realised that it had been Mum. Ian kicked again, swearing, and the motor caught. He swung the bike round in the lane and roared up after the police car, arriving in time to find Mum had just got out and was standing in front of the car in her yellow check trouser suit and giving little shrieks of protest against the cold.

Ian took off his goggles to kiss her and showed her into the house, which left Davy to watch Dad climbing slowly out of the car. He moved like an old man to stand in the lane for a while, looking up and down the valley. He sighed and shrugged, then turned to smile at Davy; but even that seemed an effort.

"Granny will be pleased to see you," said Davy, trying to make it easy for him.

"Cup of tea, Bob?" said Dad to the police driver. When the offer was accepted he had to go in too.

"I bet he's always dreamed of driving up the lane in his own Rolls," said Penny. The parents' arrival had meant a reshuffle of rooms, with Davy and Ian sharing the icy attic. Penny and Davy were up there, making the beds.

"And he'd have a bank account big enough to buy twenty new barns," she went on, "as well as colour tellies in all the bedrooms."

"I expect so," said Davy, who had in fact seen several versions of that dream during the last few years. He didn't want to talk about anything to do with poor Dad just now.

"Mum's extraordinary, isn't she?" said Penny. "She seemed to hit it off with Gran, just like that, and you wouldn't have thought they'd have anything in common at all."

"Provided she doesn't try to help with the cooking," said Davy.

"You'll have to take her for walks. Trot her up a few hills while Gran and I are cooking. Then she'll be able to eat as much as she likes, too."

Mum throve. Ian drove her once into Llangollen to buy warmer clothes, but apart from that she didn't seem at all restless. Perhaps having her own house bombed had satisfied her need for drama for a while; she was content with the old gossip of the valley, which Granny was happy to relate for hours, and could soon tell the five different Thomas families apart, which Davy had never learnt to do. She had once done half a course of evening classes in mending china, and after supper put together several old cups and tea-pots whose pieces Gran had carefully stored away. She didn't seem to miss the telly, or the beauty parlour, or Spenser Mills at all.

But Dad was moody and silent, as silent as Dadda. It wasn't just the old quarrel with Granny—they treated each other very formally. It was something to do with the explosion. Penny was probably right, Davy thought—that's how you would react if all your running and dreaming brought you to this end, back to your boyhood home in failure, with your own house rubble and the years of your manhood a meaningless waste.

On the third morning Dad went out to walk on the hills alone, brushing off Mum's puppyish attempt to go with him. He was not back by lunch when the weather, which had been cold and dry with brief powdery snow showers, changed and became a foul cold sleet out of the north-west. The visibility dropped to a few yards; the paths had changed in thirty years; he missed his way home. A stranger would have been lost altogether in the bare and houseless hills, but in late afternoon he stumbled across a remembered landmark and worked his way back in the last light, drenched and exhausted. Mum had a fine time playing hospital nurse, putting him to bed in hot blankets and feeding him gruel, but by next morning the play was real and his temperature high enough for Ian to ride down to the Prichards and telephone for the doctor. It turned out that Dad had developed a mild form of pneumonia; there was some talk of moving him to hospital, but the beds were all full in Llangollen, so in the end they decided to keep him where he was.

In the dusk of the following evening Wolf came to the farm.

10

Davy

Mum decided to go for a walk and look for birds. Davy had to go with her, for fear that she might get lost too. She marched across the hillsides with a bird-book in one hand, Ian's binoculars round her neck and a transparent umbrella held sideways to shield her complexion from the chapping wind. She was determined to see something unusual, but almost nothing moved on the drear, dun, snow-streaked slopes. At last a couple of largish birds, alarmed no doubt by the umbrella, rose and flapped sulkily away into the distance. Mum identified them as blackcock, local to rare in those parts; Davy, no puritan about birds, agreed for the sake of her pleasure, though privately he thought they were some sort of crow. Apart from them they saw nothing but a snowy owl which turned out to be a sheep-skull and a red fox which was only a rusty bit of corrugated iron. They trudged home, cheered by the blackcock.

"Look, there's a bear," said Mum.

"Honestly, Mum, they're extinct."

"Well, it could've got out of a zoo. Or somebody

might've had it for a pet and brought it out here when it got a bit too large for the flat. People can be ever so foolish."

Davy peered along the sloping flank of Moel Mawr. Already the early winter dusk was beginning to suck the colour out of the landscape, but the thing Mum had pointed at was black enough to show up sharply, a mysterious and unidentifiable shape, obviously alive. It could quite well have been a bear, but then it moved and became a cow—Bella. Bella who, for reasons only a cow would appreciate, had chosen to break out and go maundering up across the fodderless hill.

"Drat her," said Davy. "You go home, Mum. Tell Dadda I'll bring her in and milk her."

In winter Dadda kept his cows in the home paddock, where there was a shed for shelter, and ferried their fodder out to them. Even in a heavy snowfall he didn't have space to house them in the farmyard. It was typical of Bella to break out now. Probably, since Davy was out for his walk and Ian was down in Llangollen playing with the machine-guns, Dadda had simply opened the gates and called, expecting the cows to come in their accustomed turns; and Bella, who was at the low point of her milk-yield and therefore not yet uncomfortable, had taken the chance to go for a jaunt. As she was the last to be milked Dadda would be missing her about now.

Davy set off confidently across the slope, but as he came Bella moved steadily up the hill, so that in the end he had to circle right round the slate quarry before he reached her. She looked at him with an obstinate eye and tried for a while to edge past his waving arms, but at last she wheeled round and consented to be driven home.

It was almost dark by the time they reached the ridge. Davy could make out the farm only by the lights in its windows; he saw them black out one by one as Dadda went round closing the shutters. That was OK, he thought. Dadda had trusted him to cope with Bella alone; now that he had her on the downward slope he didn't expect any more trouble.

But she wasn't used to going home by this path, down at right-angles to the lane, aiming for the gate a little below the farm; she kept seeming to remember that she had an appointment elsewhere, so it was a slow process working her down; Davy had to concentrate hard on her plunging gait, ready for the least attempt to veer to one side or the other; and now she was very hard to see in the near dark, and only the upstairs lights of the farm showed for guidance.

The buzz of thought began imperceptibly, a vague oppressiveness like the beginnings of a headache or the heavy feeling that comes when the barometer drops. Then Bella suddenly remembered where she was going and surged down the last of the slope. Davy relaxed and the tide of madness washed across him.

Something had happened to Wolf. It was the same mind, but changed, changed. Some channel inside it seemed to have burst its banks so that the pictures, instead of coming one after the other, rushed out into the night in a foaming jumble. There were the lit windows of the farm, but tilted and slithering, while the black outline of the roofs pitched to and fro like ships in a storm, and over the dismal sky whirled the squiggles, black and angry, obliterating the hills. Other things blinked into being and disappeared, almost too fast to be seen—a shapeless red mass, a heavy wheel with cogs on it, the screaming face of a woman, something like a cliff falling out of the dark, veined fire, spirts of fierce colours, Mr Black Hat, a dead horse. But all the time behind this blizzard of pains the roofs and the lit windows heaved and wavered. Wolf was watching the farm.

It was like heavy snow falling on the windscreen of a car, cleared for an instant as the wiper passes but already blotting out the road ahead before the return sweep. Davy could even feel the weary effort by which Wolf prevented the blizzard from filling all his vision. Poor Wolf. Poor Wolf.

Quite unconsciously his feet had been picking their way through the ridged tussocks down to the gate, where Bella was waiting. Now the need to concentrate on untying the knotted hemp with numb fingers in the dark drove Wolf's tragic furies from his mind. Into their place flooded shock and terror. Wolf had come to the farm to kill, to slaughter everyone, to fill the rooms with blood. Davy's hands tugged uselessly at the tough shreds which seemed to stay knotted even when the main cord was loose. Dad was sick in bed, Dadda was an old man. Granny, Mum, Penny, Davy. No one could help. There was no hope.

The string gave. He heaved the gate open. Bella lurched through with Davy beside her. He did not bother to shut the gate, but in his panic rushed to head her down the lane, away from the madman in the dark; she turned, baffled, and he slapped her hard on the rump, sending her down the lane at a handsome pace. Davy, shaking all over, trotted behind her, slapping her again whenever she slowed. She was his camouflage; Wolf had no reason to suspect a boy driving a cow down the lane. Davy was going to get help, he told himself. He was going to telephone for the police from Mr Prichard's. That was the sensible thing . . . but really, he knew, he was running away.

Rather than think of that he relaxed his mind. Wolf's thoughts were faint now, but there was the lurching farm. A dim line of light gleamed towards one of the windows, a reflection off metal, a gun-barrel. They can't expect me to fight a man with a gun, he whispered. I'm right to run away, to get help. Part of him even wanted to stop, to cower, to hide in the ditch till it was all over; but, covered in cold sweat and breathing in deep, shuddering gasps, he forced his legs to run. The next time Bella sheered towards the hedge he ran straight past her, freewheeling down the slope. He started to compose in his mind what he would say to the policeman. Is that Llangollen Police Station? This is David Price from . . . There's a gunman come . . . That wouldn't do—it sounded like a hoax. They'd . . .

A motor-bike engine roared far down the hill, coughed on a gear-change, deepened to take a steeper incline. The headlight glared for a moment along the valley, swung, and at last hit the hedge of the next bend down. Davy stopped running, stepped into the middle of the lane and stood there, waving his arms. The blinding light surged up towards him. The motor cut.

"What's up?" said Ian, invisible beyond the glare.

"Wolf's at the farm!"

"Who is?"

"Wolf. You know, the man I told you about who got away from the robbery. The one who blew up our house."

"Have you seen him?"

"No, but. . ."

"Look, Davy . . ."

It was too late to lie now.

"*I know* he's there," cried Davy. "I can't tell you how but I know!"

Ian was still screened by the wall of light, but Davy knew from the tone of his voice what his face would look like, in the uneasy zone between kindness and contempt.

"Look, kid, you've been having a rough time, getting Dad out of his mess, and then the bomb at the house and now this pneumonia. Just relax. Take it easy. The guy couldn't be here. The fuzz wouldn't have told anyone where they were taking Dad, would they?"

"That piece in the *Examiner.* Mr Boland put the address in."

"Hell, he wouldn't have seen that."

"He's got a gun, Ian."

"You haven't *seen* him, kid."

"Well, I'm going down to Prichard's to ring up the police."

"You're bloody well not."

"You can't stop me. He's there, I tell you. He's there. He'll kill them all. He's like that."

Ian was fiddling with the controls in an indecisive way. Davy could hear the throttle cable sigh and click.

"OK," said Ian suddenly. "I'll go and get someone."

"He really has got a gun. And he's quite mad. He's very dangerous."

Ian only grunted and swung the bike away so that at last Davy was out of the glare, but still too night-blinded to see his brother when he hesitated again.

"You coming?"

"Perhaps I'd better. Then I can persuade them . . ."

"You haven't persuaded *me*," grumbled Ian. All at once he seemed to make his mind up.

"You stay here," he said. "Don't do anything stupid. I shan't be long."

He pushed off and allowed the bike to sidle down the hill. Davy ran a few steps after him, stopped and watched the tail-light vanish round the bend. He stood in the road, panting, and allowed his night vision to come back to him. It was very dark now, even so.

He could still run down to Prichard's and telephone

the police. But that was another two miles, and by
then Ian would be back with his Nationalist friends,
with guns. The police wouldn't come armed, not for
a telephone call from an excited boy—but if they did
come, and found Ian and his friends there, what would
Ian think? He had shown a sort of trust, going off for
Davy on what he clearly thought was a crazy errand,
but if Davy betrayed him Ian would never trust him
again. It was better to leave it to the Nationalists.

And that meant that Davy could go back and warn
them at the farm that Wolf was there. He could have
done this in the first place, if he hadn't panicked.
Seeing Wolf's thoughts would allow Davy to keep
away from him, to get in on the other side . . .

Slowly, reluctant with the fear of what he must face,
he started back up the road. Far down the hill he heard
Ian's motor start; then, as if that had been a signal,
clamour rose from the farm.

Rud's savage burst of barking was cut short by a
louder noise, three or four sharp, slamming explosions.
A man shouted. A door crashed shut. Glass broke.

Davy was running back up the lane. He was afraid
still, but the need for action mastered his terror. Ian
would be back with his friends in twenty minutes.
One or two minutes gained by any kind of diversion
might make all the difference.

In the black shadow of the hedge a blacker shadow
shuffled. Davy stopped, heart bouncing. Bella. He
dithered for a moment, but the noise of her reminded
him that it was no use getting there with a clatter of

shoes and loud, gasping breath. Wolf would hear him, and he'd be too tired to be any use. He walked on carefully, using the verge where he could, trying to still the harsh breath that came and went through his throat. The slope began to ease. He was nearly there, so he stopped to try to think; but once he had stopped fear locked him. He could not force himself to face it.

More glass broke. A window creaked and Dadda's voice called out, "You there! You cannot get in. My shutters are good oak and I have a shotgun in my hand up here."

Silence and dark. Davy shut his eyes and waited. For a moment he saw nothing, but then into his mind blazed a pillar of pure light, a clean crack in the blackness; a couple of squiggles whirled across it; a curve of blue edged into the pillar from the left, then drifted out again; next a dark brown vertical line edged in from the right. That vanished and the blue curve showed again.

This time Davy knew what it was, a bit of the souvenir plate from Bangor that hung on the parlour wall; the brown line had been the edge of the door-frame. Wolf was peeping through the thin crack between the shutters of the little side window that looked up the valley—so it would be safe to go at least as far as the farmyard. He could hide there, spy on Wolf's mind, and do what he could to help, if he dared. He stole up towards the gateway.

The pillar vanished. More glass broke. In a panic Davy dodged round the gatepost and into the total blackness under the tractor shed. Fear so filled his mind that for some moments he could not see what Wolf was thinking about, but then came an image of fire, the pitching roof-lines burning, flames at the doors, Dad running out into the orange glare and being gunned down. The sequence came two or three times, almost untroubled by squiggles, and was followed by a picture of a bright blue tractor, shiny as a toy. Beside the tractor was a bright yellow jerrican.

Dadda's tractor had once been as blue as that, though now it was patched and mottled with age; and beside it, at the front of the tractor shed, he kept a rusty jerrican of the paraffin on which it ran. Almost with relief Davy seized the chance to do something, to achieve a moment of delay. He felt his way up the far side of the tractor, found the jerrican and carried it quietly back until he could settle it inside the big rear wheel of the tractor, right under the axle. Even by daylight you'd have to bend down to spot it there.

Davy moved round the tractor and nestled against its further side. The night was going to get no darker now; by straining his sight he could distinguish a few objects out in the open yard, the milk-churn stand and the huge tractor tyre that had leaned for the last five years against the white asbestos wall of the generator shed. He would have liked to move to different cover, but Wolf was nearer now and Davy thought he might spot him, or hear him, if he tried to run.

Wolf came in silence, holding firm in the storm of his mind to the image of the yellow can standing

against the tarred clapboarding of the wall. He must
have spotted it, Davy thought, spying out the farm in
the last light, after Dadda had finished milking and
before he took Rud out for his final check-round.
Davy, crouched with one hand on the front wheel of
the tractor, felt a slight jar as something bumped
against the far tyre. Wolf was able to recall exactly
where he had seen the can, a fixed certainty among
the upheavals of his mind. Then Davy heard a
low grunt and the picture of the can blanked out.
The tractor shed filled with a low, bubbling snarl
as the furious black squiggles smothered Wolf's
mind, pulsing like swarmed bees; it must have been a
minute before he managed to wipe them away and
tried to reconstruct his image of the can. It came
unsteadily, shifting its colour and outline and position.
Davy could hear shufflings and gropings. As the
squiggles began to whirl across the unsteady image
Davy felt the man's misery and despair run through
him like a current.

"Poor Wolf," he said, aloud.

Everything stopped, the noise of groping, the
misery, the raging thoughts. What Davy could see in
his mind was what he could see with his eyes, the total
blackness of the tractor shed, through which Wolf was
trying to peer. Suddenly Davy remembered his real
name.

"Poor Dick," he said gently.

He heard a grunt, but no snarl. All Wolf's mind was
busy with the effort of searching for whoever had

spoken. Then a picture formed, a slab-faced man in uniform with a sort of truncheon in his hand.

"No," said Davy. "I'm not him. I won't hurt you, Dick."

The picture blanked out and became the dark of the shed.

In the long pause that followed Davy began to realize what he had done. The gift, linking him to Wolf, forcing him to share some of the man's rage and sorrow, had betrayed him into speaking aloud. But Wolf would not understand that. He had come to the farm to kill.

There was a light scratching noise, twice repeated. Just as he recognised what it was the match burst into light.

For an instant the flare was like sunrise, too brilliant to see by. But as his pupils narrowed he saw Wolf's face, above and to one side of the match, deep-shadowed and ghastly. The skin was filthy with mud and sweat and there was a bloody cut on one cheek-bone. The cheeks themselves were grey and hollow. The eyes had sunk back into their sockets and were very bloodshot. Several days' bristle grew along the jaw.

So appalling was this gaunt, exhausted face that not until the match burnt Wolf's fingers and he dropped it with an oath did Davy think of looking for the gun in the other hand, and then it was too late. They had simply stood there, staring at each other, face to face for the first time. And now that he had seen him looking like that, Davy's pity for Wolf stopped being something that existed only in the half-real world of the gift. It became part of the solid, outside world, like his terror.

In the new dark he saw Wolf's image of him, sly and pasty-faced and treacherous, with the points of his two lower canine teeth showing outside his upper lip.

"That's not me," he said. "I'm Davy. I won't hurt you."

Black squiggles began to dart into the picture.

"Send them away," said Davy quietly. "Send them away, Dick."

Boy and squiggles were wiped out, and instead there was a much more realistic picture of Davy, carefully registered in his exact position as he crouched by the front wheel. Still crouching Davy moved forward, sliding close by the radiator so that his shape would not show against the faint light from the entrance. At such close quarters as this he could actually sense where Wolf's thoughts were coming from, and mark his stealthy progress round behind the tractor.

It would be a bad idea, Davy realised, to let Wolf get as far as where he had been standing and experience the frustration and fury of a missed blow.

"You're tired, Dick, aren't you?" he said. "And you're hungry."

He had to keep his voice calm and easy, despite the strain and fear. But here the gift helped, allowing him to feel and share Wolf's exhaustion and hunger as well as his despairing rage. Wolf swore again at the sound of his voice, but in a vague, almost emotionless fashion. Furthermore he stayed where he was, leaning against the tractor's rear wheel-guard.

"I 'aven't 'ad a bite two days," he said suddenly. Apart from the two oaths those were the first words he'd spoken. His voice was deep and soft, but with a whining note in it which might have come from hunger or might have been habit.

"I could get you a mug of milk," said Davy.

Wolf made a grunting noise of acceptance.

"OK," said Davy. "You wait here."

He longed to run, to dart sideways out of any line of fire. Instead he forced himself to walk steadily across the yard towards the milk-shed door. He turned on the light—most of the farm lights were out so there was no danger of straining the accumulators—and the important thing was to be quick, not to leave Wolf alone long enough for him to remember why he had come, perhaps even to realise that Davy must have moved the jerrican. Dadda liked milk and kept a white enamel mug in the milk-shed and sterilised it with the other equipment. He dipped this into a half-filled churn, turned the light off and walked quietly back across the yard. As he came he realised that Wolf had moved almost out into the open and had, even in those few seconds, already been alone too long with his thoughts. His mind was full of the swarming squiggles, whose abstract rage was as much a hatred of himself as of the world that had made him like he was. Poor Wolf. Poor Dick.

Davy halted and licked his lips before he dared to speak.

"Send them away, Dick," he called. "I've brought your milk. Send them away."

The picture convulsed, staggered and was gone, replaced by the lurching darkness of the yard with a human shape standing vague in the middle.

"That's better," said Davy. "Here's your milk. I'll put it on the tractor for you."

He walked delicately forward, poised for any warning flicker in the mad mind. If he had to run he hoped his own knowledge of the farmyard might allow him to beat Wolf's speed and strength. He would race for the gap between Granny's hen-house and the feed-store and slip through; he thought Wolf would be too bulky to follow. But now Wolf's mind was thinking about milk, and hunger, and cold, and the dreadful dark. Davy kept the bulk of the tractor between the two of them and settled the mug on the metal, holding it steady until Wolf's groping hand found it. In the process their fingers touched. Wolf's seemed as cold and hard as the iron itself. Davy had his ears cocked for the first far sound of Ian's bike taking the inclines. He'd leave it far down the lane and walk up. Or perhaps his friends would bring him by car. In either case it would be dangerous for them to come with Wolf in this natural ambush by the farmyard gate. The noise of Wolf's swallowing ceased.

"Ah," he said. "Any more where that came from?"

"Gallons," said Davy. "You can have as much as you

like. And it's warmer in the milk-shed, too. You bring the mug."

He walked quickly off across the yard without looking back. As soon as he was in the milk-shed he flicked the light on and scampered half way up the stairs to the hay loft. His idea was that on an instant of warning from Wolf's mind he'd be able to race up into the musty dark, across the cloying hay and down the far ladder by feel, leaving Wolf wallowing.

But Wolf stood hesitating by the door. Again his mind was filled with the image of that slab-faced man with the black truncheon, this time waiting hidden behind the door of the shed.

"It's all right," called Davy. "It's only me. He's not here."

Wolf moved blinking into the light. Tiredness had not changed that strange, poised walk. He clutched the mug in one large hand and from the other dangled a big black pistol.

"You know the bastard?" he said.

"No," said Davy.

"You're lucky," said Wolf.

"The milk's in that churn there," said Davy. "Just dip in."

Wolf did so. He was drinking his third mugful when he suddenly tensed, with his pistol up. In his mind the dark crystal-veined calm was replaced by the glaring shed, with shapes prowling in the outside dark. Davy heard something shift and rustle beyond the partition.

"It's all right," said Davy. "It's only a cow, Bella. She

broke out and didn't get milked, so she's come for it now."

"Yeah," said Wolf. "A cow. That's right. I always wanted a cow of my own."

But his pistol was still pointing at the dark.

"Would you like to see her?" said Davy.

He nipped down the stair, opened the half-door into the milking stalls and slipped back to his perch. All Wolf's mind was taken up with Bella, who, inquisitive even by the normal standards of cows, had immediately poked her head into the light to see what was going on. She started to scratch the underside of her jaw on the rough top of the door.

"'Ullo, old lady," said Wolf.

The warm, slightly acid cow-odour breathed across into the milk-shed. Wolf put his mug down, walked across and with a firm but gentle hand teased the hummock on Bella's head where the horns should have grown. Bella enjoyed it for a few moments, but she was restless with her need to be milked and desire for her bit of cattle-cake, and suddenly she backed away. Davy had been watching her through Wolf's mind, where her eyes were great violet pools and her hide as soft as the fur of a black cat. Now he saw how her solemn gentleness, followed by her refusal of Wolf's caress, hurt like a whip. The picture changed to a brown cow lying by a road with her flank sliced open and a tangle of innards showing. The pistol rose.

"Dick," whispered Davy. "Tell me about Trevor, Dick."

It was the best he could think of. Wolf hesitated, trapped by the worshipped name. He looked round the milk-shed with a frown and suddenly remembered why he was at the farm at all.

"Where's that Price bloke?" he said fiercely. "Trev said to do him. Sent me a message out of nick."

"Mr Price is very ill," said Davy. "He got lost on the hill in a storm and now he's got pneumonia."

"Done for?" asked Wolf

"I don't know," said Davy. "The doctor said it was very serious."

"That's right," said Wolf. "Mucking old Trev about like that. Pneumonia done for my grand-dad."

Davy saw a picture of a wizened old man with a bluish face; he had a thick strap coiled round his right fist.

"What's the belt for?" said Davy to keep the conversation going.

"Lay into me with," said Wolf. "'E was a cruel one, bad drunk and worse sober. Pneumonia done for 'im too. That's right."

Wolf seemed to accept without question Davy's ability to see into his mind—it might be something to do with the way his horrible imaginings were just as real to him as the outer world. Now he stood gazing at the half-door, where Bella was scratching her jaw again with a steady, rasping rhythm.

"Always fancied a cow of my own," he muttered. "Found a dog, once, when I was a kid, but they took him away and drowned him. I like dogs. Pity about that other one. Shouldn't of gone for me."

"Rud?" said Davy.

"I dunno 'is name. Shouldn't of gone for me, but the old bloke let 'im."

Davy swallowed and forced himself to think and talk as though all that were something in a story.

"What happened?" he said.

"Shot 'im, I suppose," said Wolf, gesturing vaguely with the gun as though it were a thing with a will of its own. "The old bloke ran inside. 'E shouldn't of gone for me."

"I'm sorry," said Davy. "He couldn't help it. It's what he'd been trained to do."

"Vicious, that is," said Wolf, "learning a dog to go for a bloke. Got any more of that milk?"

"Help yourself," said Davy.

Wolf settled his pistol on the ledge where Dadda kept his cow medicines. He still looked very tired, but there was something less tense and wary about his walk as he went to the churn, dipped the mug and settled on Dadda's old milking-stool to sip slowly. Davy was worried about Ian, worried about how long he had been and also about what would happen when he came back. Wolf seemed so quiet now, so manageable—but if those silly Nationalists came charging in with guns . . . and besides, the reason why Wolf was quiet and manageable was that he was learning to trust Davy, to treat him as a friend—but Davy, by keeping him calm and unsuspecting, was all the time betraying that trust. It was the only thing to do, but that made it no less shameful.

He watched through Wolf's eyes the various whites of the empty mug where the dim yellow light from the naked bulb sent a shadowed parabola across the inner surface. Into this purity swam a whirling squiggle, and then another.

"Send them away, Dick," said Davy. "Send them away. You can do it."

Wolf looked up. He saw the whitewashed walls of the milk-shed almost as they were, not wavering or lurching, and the dark diagonal of the worn old stair where Davy sat, and Davy himself, a very fine kid, large-eyed and clear-skinned, and clever with it—the sort of kid a bloke could get along with all right . . .

"Them worms—you get 'em too?" said Wolf.

Davy hesitated.

"I call them squiggles," he said.

"Yeah. That's right. Once told Trev 'ow they bothered me, but 'e only laughed."

"Poor Dick," said Davy. "They're bad, aren't they?"

"That's right—but I can't do nothing for 'em."

"But there's something else," said Davy. "It's sort of dark, with white veins across it."

Wolf immediately made a picture of it.

"That's right," he said. "That's me marble job. Like a bit of pretty stone, see? Good, innit?"

"It's peaceful," said Davy.

"That's right," said Wolf

They looked at each other, bound by a cord of trust.

Davy didn't know what to do. He was sure that doctors could help Wolf, with drugs or somehow, if only he could be persuaded to try. Davy would have to do that, using the trust between them to keep Wolf safe and calm. The first thing was to get him food and persuade him to sleep in the hay-loft, and then explain to Dadda. Dadda would understand because he knew about the gift. But the police . . . you couldn't expect the police to stop thinking of Wolf as a dangerous criminal with a record of violence, just because a boy said he could be trusted now . . .

Wolf was looking at Davy as he used to look at Mr Black Hat, with a kind of worship. Davy didn't like it. Uncomfortable, he stood up.

"Now, Dick . . ." he began.

"All right," snapped Ian's voice at the door, "put your hands up."

Wolf sprang from the stool with that ugly, bubbling snarl which Davy had heard when he lost the jerrican. His hand flashed to his jacket pocket.

"It's all right, Dick," said Davy urgently. "It's all right."

But already the cord of trust was broken.

"I said put your hands up," said Ian, walking into the light, with the squat machine-gun steady at his hip. He looked monstrous in his leathers and goggles and that was how Wolf saw him, a black predator, a creature of night, not human at all. Wolf paid no attention to the order to put his hands up. His mind was filled with flashes of the night-monster and crimson explosions and sharp, realistic images of the missing gun. The walls of the milk-shed reeled and threatened. Suddenly, beside the gun, Wolf summoned up a picture of the medicine bottles.

Davy leaped down the stairs and snatched the gun off the shelf. As Wolf with unbelievable quickness sprang across the shed towards him he flung it out over Ian's shoulder into the dark. Its safety-catch must have been off, for just as Wolf's rush bashed Davy headlong against the wall it hit the ground and fired. Davy crouched, head ringing. Wolf swung round, lowered his head like a charging bull, cuffed Ian out of the way with a back-handed flip and plunged out into the dark. Ian switched the light out.

"Huw wouldn't give me any ammo," said Ian in a stupid voice. "Sorry, Dave. I didn't think it mattered."

Davy shook his head, trying to clear it from the whirlpool of dark nothings that pulsed through Wolf's mind as he staggered grunting round the yard, searching for his weapon.

"Stand clear, boys," called Dadda's voice from an upper window. The night was seared by another shot. Davy heard a few pellets that must have ricocheted off a flagstone rattle against the hen-house. The hens squawked sleepily. Wolf snarled in the dark.

"Don't shoot," called Davy desperately. "Don't shoot, Dadda. Dick's all right, aren't you, Dick?"

But the cord of trust could not be tied again. At the sound of Davy's voice Wolf stood still and swore; he raised his head to Dadda's window and shouted, no words but a racking wail. It lasted several seconds before he wheeled away and plunged out into the dark.

"Don't be an idiot, Dave!" shouted Ian.

Davy didn't hear him. He was already half across the yard. He could see only what Wolf was seeing, and there the shapes of the dark were almost obliterated by the storm-cloud of fears and furies; but he sensed the rush down the lane, the hesitation at the shadowed tunnel between the hedges, the glimpse of the paler slope beyond the open gate, the outline of the ridge.

Davy paused at the gate.

"Dick!" he called. "Dick!"

The only response was that the storm-cloud thickened, so that even the ridge-line vanished. Blind now, Wolf stumbled on.

Wolf was strong and quick, but he was tired. Davy's legs were used to the hills. They kept pace, stumbling among ridges and tussocks. The winter air rattled in Davy's throat. His blood thundered. He staggered on, following, like a hound on the trail, the frenzied centre of that storm of darkness. He was reeling when, all of a sudden, like lightning against a thundercloud, a jagged prong of fire lanced through the black. He yelled with the felt pain of it. Ian's voice answered, somewhere down in the dark.

And then Davy's mind was clear and he was still struggling up the hill through the ordinary dark. Ian called again, but Davy had no breath to answer. Perhaps the cloud layer had thinned, or the moon was up behind it, but now he could see enough to pick out bushes and boulders, and from the shape of the skyline tell that he was heading towards the slate quarry. Cautiously he dropped to all fours and crawled on, but even so he reached the cliff sooner than he had expected.

He gulped, and shivered in the night wind, as he knelt there staring down at the black levels below.

"Dick!" he called. "Dick!"

Nothing happened. He called again and again, working his way leftward along the cliff edge, pausing between shouts for any answer except his own voice echoing off the cliffs. All at once a little explosion of darkness rose in his mind, veined with red fire. It burst and was gone. But it meant that Wolf was not dead; he had fallen over the cliff edge and was lying down there in the darkness, hurt and unconscious. Davy looked over his shoulder down the hill, wondering whether to go for help.

A beam of light wavered by the farm, pointed down the lane for a moment, then swung and glared across the slope; faint against the wind Davy could hear the deep note of the tractor engine. He rose and walked back the way he had come, to where a small subsidiary ridge stretched sideways from the quarry lip, and walked out along it. When you were at the farm, this seemed to be the highest point of the hill.

The tractor rose from a dip which had hidden it and came weaving up the slope, its two fierce lights slashing from side to side. Davy waited till they were almost on him, then waved both arms above his head several times. The path of the tractor steadied and it surged up the hill straight towards him. Ian jumped down and ran across, leaving the motor running.

"You're a blazing idiot," he shouted. "Where's the bloke? I found his pistol. Dadda's driven down to phone for the fuzz."

"He's fallen in the quarry," said Davy urgently. "But he isn't dead yet. Can you get the tractor round to the bottom?"

"I'm not going down there if he's alive," said Ian, "and nor are you. How do you know?"

"Like I knew he was at the farm," said Davy, snarly with exhaustion.

"OK, OK," said Ian. "I'll run her on to that bit of slope and then she'll shine over most of it."

Twice during the manœuvrings Davy experienced the same momentary explosions of Wolf's consciousness, veined with fiery pain, but there was no point in trying to shout to him above the racket of the engine. And then, though the tractor was poised with chocked wheels on a sharp slope at the very lip of the cliffs, its lights only shone over half the levels.

Davy turned, determined to run along the edge of the quarry until he could climb down to its floor, but at that moment the black, fire-streaked turmoil rose in his mind, strong and persisting.

"He's there!" he said, pointing into the pitch darkness where the highest level ran. "Dick! Dick!"

The rocks sent back the name, thinned by the breeze. The shadow of the cliff on which they stood ran in a jagged arc along the tumbled screes. Their own shadows, spindly with stretching, reached across the pocked grey slopes and flats. Davy stared at the blank arena through the blizzard in his mind.

"There!" he shouted. "There!"

"There," wailed the cliffs.

Out of the black centre of the arc crawled a shape. Its shadow looked solider than itself. It moved with a pain that Davy could feel fiery along his own nerves. It dragged one leg. It crossed the small ledge of level by the ruins of the big shed. Slowly it came to where the longest of the screes of spoil spilt down in one tumbled diagonal towards the further darkness. When it reached the edge of the scree it crawled on without a pause.

At once it began to slither, head foremost. About twelve feet down it lodged for a moment against a projecting wedge of stone, but its weight shifted that and it went slithering on while the rocks of the scree, dislodged by the movement of the wedge, loosed themselves from where they had lain so long and began to tumble after it. Now the whole scree was sliding, freed from the very top, tearing back yards of the edge of the tip, avalanching into the dark with a low, harsh rumble. Over it all grey slate-dust rose like smoke.

Wolf was invisible, but the storm of his pain filled the whole night, making Davy yell, stagger and clutch at Ian to stay upright.

Then it was gone, wiped clean. He fell to his knees choking back vomit. A soft dark swallowed him.

11

Dick

"You can't expect everything to be all right, just like that," said Penny. "It doesn't happen."

Davy said nothing, but stared down into the quarry. The real snow had come, heavy and soft. Only the dark blue cliffs resisted the smothering whiteness, too vertical for the snow to settle; but even they were softened with mottling patches where a cranny or ledge had accepted the snow flakes. The levels below, and the roofless sheds, and the screes were all now remoulded into peaceful, colourless, round-edged mounds and planes, except where the wind had carved the drifts into sharp shapes.

"There's more pluses than minuses," said Penny. She started numbering them off. "Dad's better, and if the firm's really found us a new house, like the man said, it looks as though he's going to keep his job; I know Granny hasn't really made it up with him, but there's a chance of it now; and no one got hurt or killed, except Rud, and it might have been all of us. The only minuses are Rud and Wolf."

"He thought he could trust me," said Davy.

11

Dick

"You can't expect everything to be all right, just like that," said Penny. "It doesn't happen."

Davy said nothing, but stared down into the quarry. The real snow had come, heavy and soft. Only the dark blue cliffs resisted the smothering whiteness, too vertical for the snow to settle; but even they were softened with mottling patches where a cranny or ledge had accepted the snow flakes. The levels below, and the roofless sheds, and the screes were all now remoulded into peaceful, colourless, round-edged mounds and planes, except where the wind had carved the drifts into sharp shapes.

"There's more pluses than minuses," said Penny. She started numbering them off. "Dad's better, and if the firm's really found us a new house, like the man said, it looks as though he's going to keep his job; I know Granny hasn't really made it up with him, but there's a chance of it now; and no one got hurt or killed, except Rud, and it might have been all of us. The only minuses are Rud and Wolf."

"He thought he could trust me," said Davy.

ran in a jagged arc along the tumbled screes. Their
own shadows, spindly with stretching, reached across
the pocked grey slopes and flats. Davy stared at the
blank arena through the blizzard in his mind.

"There!" he shouted. "There!"

"There," wailed the cliffs.

Out of the black centre of the arc crawled a shape.
Its shadow looked solider than itself. It moved with a
pain that Davy could feel fiery along his own nerves. It
dragged one leg. It crossed the small ledge of level by
the ruins of the big shed. Slowly it came to where the
longest of the screes of spoil spilt down in one tumbled
diagonal towards the further darkness. When it reached
the edge of the scree it crawled on without a pause.

At once it began to slither, head foremost. About
twelve feet down it lodged for a moment against a
projecting wedge of stone, but its weight shifted that
and it went slithering on while the rocks of the scree,
dislodged by the movement of the wedge, loosed
themselves from where they had lain so long and began
to tumble after it. Now the whole scree was sliding,
freed from the very top, tearing back yards of the edge
of the tip, avalanching into the dark with a low, harsh
rumble. Over it all grey slate-dust rose like smoke.

Wolf was invisible, but the storm of his pain filled
the whole night, making Davy yell, stagger and clutch
at Ian to stay upright.

Then it was gone, wiped clean. He fell to his knees
choking back vomit. A soft dark swallowed him.

passage to make the going easier for herself. She stopped and looked back.

"If a tracker followed us," she said, "he'd think we were a cow in gumboots."

Davy laughed, not because of the joke but because she was taking the trouble to try and cheer him up. And in fact, when they did go on, he found it easier to bear his misery and his breaking of Dick's trust. Usually you could walk from the quarry to the cairn in a bit over thirty minutes. This time it took them more than an hour, but they found the snow shallower near the summit because the wind up there had been too strong to let it settle as thickly as it had on the sheltered slopes. A long tapering tail of snow had drifted sideways from the cairn itself. They shuffled round in circles on the bitter top, trying to feel for stones with their feet. Soon any hardened lump of trodden snow felt much the same as a chunk of stone.

"We should have brought them up from the quarry," said Davy.

"Through this?" said Penny. "No thanks. I've got one here."

The next two came quickly, but it took them ages to find the fourth. Davy wouldn't give up and Penny, marvellously, didn't suggest it, though she must have been very numb and hungry. She's right about people liking each other, Davy thought. That's what matters. Suddenly, fetching a wider circle away from the cairn, he stubbed his toe on something under one of the scrubby bits of heather that grew here and there on its own strange way; it had altered the shape of the hill for ever. Dick had done the same to Davy. There was no forgetting him.

Sound travels a long way over a winter valley. They heard Ian's shout from the farm, faint and clear. He was standing just above the lane in his red anorak, waving his arms, telling them to come home.

"That's all right," said Penny. "They've found them all. I never thought there'd be any up here."

(Some of the sheep had been out on the hillside when the blizzard had come. As soon as the weather had cleared everyone who could move on the farm had trudged out to look for them, in case they had huddled into shelter where some trick of the storm had smothered them in a drift. Penny and Davy were supposed to be checking the ridge.)

"You go down," said Davy. "I'm going up to the cairn."

"Didn't you hear Dadda say? We can't go tomorrow. The lane won't be cleared for at least two days."

Davy shrugged and turned along the lip of the quarry. It was tiresome walking. You either had to scuffle your feet forward through the snow or lift them right clear; and in places the snow had a dip in the ground where you could sink above your knees. The quarry edge curved away. He stopped to rest.

"Get on, Wenceslas," said Penny.

The crunch and rustle of his movements had drowned the noise of hers; she had been picking her way along his footprints, taking advantage of his it was like that when he was alive. Nobody wanted to know, except Mr Black Hat a bit, and then me."

"I think they're right. You've got to forget him too."

Davy shook his head.

"There'll be somebody else," said Penny. "Look, there might even be somebody with the same sort of trouble, something wrong with his brain like that but not so dangerous, and you could help him. If you could see what Wolf was thinking . . ."

"That's all gone," said Davy.

"Are you sure?"

"I think so. He took it with him when he went down the scree. I felt it go. It was something to do with the pain."

"It might come back."

"No."

"Well, that's another plus," said Penny. "You've always wanted to get shot of it. Now you can be just like anybody else."

"Nobody's like anybody else."

"Oh, for heaven's sake! You know what I mean."

But even so it wasn't true, Davy thought. You are what you are, and you are what you do, and you are what happens to you. Dick had happened to Davy and by that alone he was different. The snow would cover the hills, and go; the screes of spoil would lie where they had been tipped year after year. Wolf would lie with them, spoil too, a waste product, thrown away. The quarry was part of the hillside now, beautiful in

"It wasn't your fault. If you hadn't got his gun he'd have killed Ian and you too, and probably the rest of us after."

"He needed me. He had to have someone like me, someone who treated him as a person, and not just as a dangerous dog. I let him down."

"But he'd always have been like a dangerous dog with other people, even if he was safe with you. *I* don't think doctors could have done much for him—not, you know, made him properly human. They might have been able to keep him stupid and sleepy, that's all."

"He never had a chance," said Davy. "We think we've had a rough time, Pen, being mucked around by Mum and Dad and never having a proper home and all that, but compared with him . . ."

"We all like each other," said Penny. "That's what matters. Even Ian likes Mum and you and me—and there's been Granny and Dadda too. I mean, look at Dad—he's done some crazy things, but people aren't only what they do. What they do's important, but they aren't only that."

"He wasn't," said Davy, gazing down at the white slant that hid the scree.

"Are they going to dig him out?"

"Too dangerous, that policeman said. I don't know. They don't really want to think about him. I mean, if he'd been alive and they'd caught him, they couldn't have tried him like Mr Black Hat and the others. So now . . . well, it's easiest for them just to forget him. They're going to pretend he never happened. I suppose